Better Homes and Gardens®
KITCHEN
IDEA FILE

Meredith® Books
Des Moines, Iowa

Better Homes and Gardens® Kitchen Idea File
Editor: Vicki Christian
Contributing Project Manager/Writer: Catherine M. Staub, Lexicon Consulting, Inc.
Contributing Editor/Writer: Julie Collins, Lexicon Consulting, Inc.
Contributing Graphic Designer: David Jordan, Studio 22
Copy Chief: Terri Fredrickson
Publishing Operations Manager: Karen Schirm
Senior Editor, Asset & Information Management: Phillip Morgan
Edit and Design Production Coordinator: Mary Lee Gavin
Editorial Assistant: Kaye Chabot
Book Production Managers: Pam Kvitne, Marjorie J. Schenkelberg, Rick von Holdt, Mark Weaver
Contributing Copy Editor: Linda Armstrong
Contributing Proofreaders: Dan J. Degen, Sara Henderson, Ann Narue Sapienza
Contributing Cover Photographer: Emily Followill
Contributing Indexer: Jana Finnegan

Meredith® Books
Executive Director, Editorial: Gregory H. Kayko
Executive Director, Design: Matt Strelecki
Managing Editor: Amy Tincher-Durik
Senior Editor/Group Manager: Vicki Leigh Ingham
Marketing Product Manager: Steve Rogers

Publisher and Editor in Chief: James D. Blume
Editorial Director: Linda Raglan Cunningham
Executive Director, Marketing: Steve Malone
Executive Director, New Business Development: Todd M. Davis
Executive Director, Sales: Ken Zagor
Director, Operations: George A. Susral
Director, Production: Douglas M. Johnston
Director, Marketing: Amy Nichols
Business Director: Jim Leonard

Vice President and General Manager: Douglas J. Guendel

Better Homes and Gardens® **Magazine**
Deputy Editor, Home Design: Oma Blaise Ford

Meredith Publishing Group
President: Jack Griffin
Executive Vice President: Bob Mate

Meredith Corporation
Chairman and Chief Executive Officer: William T. Kerr
President and Chief Operating Officer: Stephen M. Lacy

In Memoriam: E.T. Meredith III (1933–2003)

All of us at Meredith® Books are dedicated to providing you with information and ideas to enhance your home. We welcome your comments and suggestions. Write to us at: Meredith Books, Home Decorating and Design Editorial Department, 1716 Locust St., Des Moines, IA 50309-3023.

Somewhere out there, your dream kitchen awaits.

Perhaps you've been researching, tearing pages from magazines, and making note of kitchen elements you like. Or maybe you're just getting started, and inspiration has yet to strike. Regardless, in this book you'll find ideas to get you headed in the right direction.

Inspiration for Planning Your Kitchen Design

The shape and size of your kitchen—from a generously proportioned U-shape cooking area to a tiny galley-style space—impact everything from where you situate appliances to how you decorate. Whether you're considering a simple update with fresh colors and accessories or a substantial kitchen remodeling or addition, look here first for ideas to jump-start your planning process.

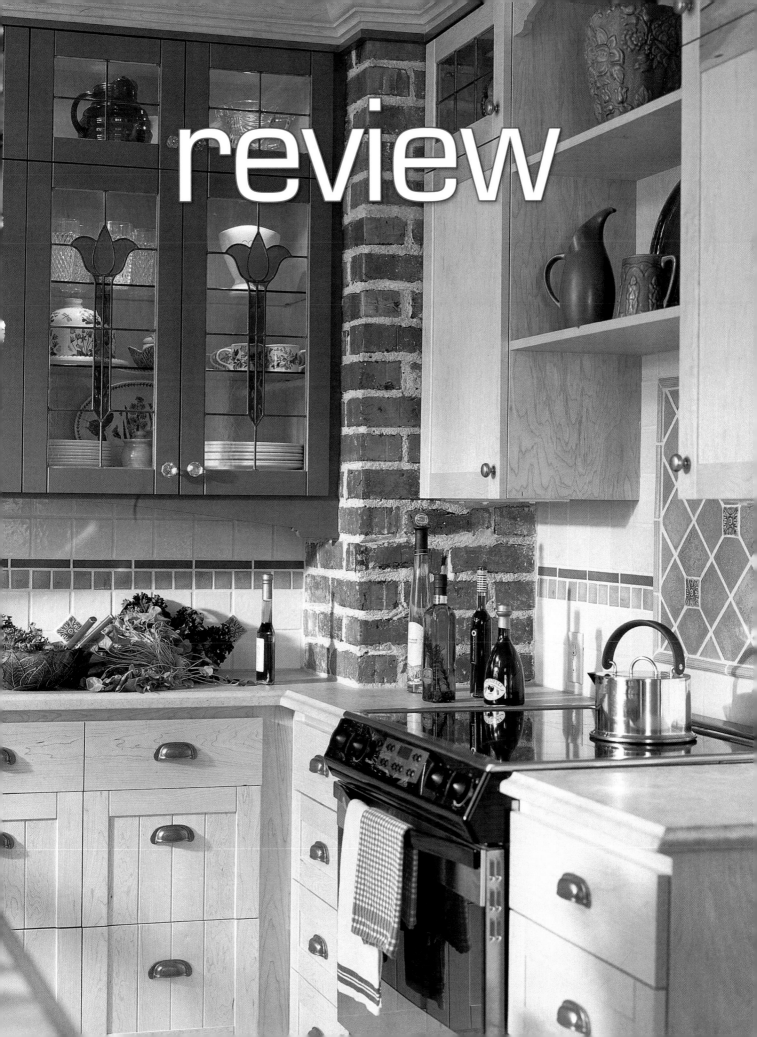

review

Crowd Control

No matter where in the house they are served, guests like the kitchen. Instead of wanting a large kitchen with room for guests, however, these homeowners chose to enclose a modest-size space and encourage company to gather in other parts of the home. Changing the layout from a long, open U to a nearly closed C keeps the kitchen self-contained but functional. A pass-through ensures guests mingling in the living room aren't closed off from the cooks, and a second doorway eases traffic flow. To squeeze every drop of utility from the 175-square-foot room, a pantry provides prep space. A hutch and custom cabinets with drawers all the way to the floor provide more storage. The finished kitchen proves that sometimes downsizing creates a cozy kitchen that's just right.

1: With such a small kitchen, guests stay out of the way in the living room. A pass-through keeps the kitchen from feeling closed off and makes serving during parties easier.

2: The pantry built next to the oven wall maximizes every inch of space and even includes a small sink and plenty of electrical outlets for appliances.

3: A banquette seating area just outside the cooking space provides an intimate spot for family meals.

4: Glass doors in the built-in hutch near the island showcase a collection of mid-20th-century pottery.

Rustic Fare

This newly built kitchen captures the countryside sensibility of a neighborly gathering place. Any true gourmand would love the power of a professional cooking space and styling reminiscent of the generous traditions of rural life.

Evoking the spaciousness of an old barn, vaulted ceilings soar above the broad kitchen and draw attention to the wrought-iron chandelier that hangs above the central island. Furniture-like cabinets suggest a simple, rural sensibility and display the weathered red finish of a traditional barn. Rustic inspiration is also evident in the island, which boasts a farmhouse-style limestone sink surrounded by a rich walnut countertop.

Unlike a traditional farm kitchen, however, this space was designed for large-scale entertaining and cooking projects. Workstations loaded with storage cater to every task. The 8-foot-long island, which serves as the kitchen's centerpiece, includes ample storage and prep space and is frequently used as a buffet. Each side of the kitchen features an extra workstation, complete with a cutting board and refrigerator drawers. A butler's pantry with storage, a full refrigerator, and a double wall oven create a second cooking area with even more country style.

1: Tucked behind a side door, the charming butler's pantry is a fully functional kitchen on its own.

2: The sun-filled space accommodates large-scale entertaining, as well as multiple cooks, with the central island and fully loaded work spaces.

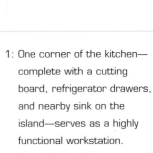

SITUATION

- Multiple cooks required gourmet conveniences and plenty of space for tackling major projects.
- Although the kitchen was new, the homeowners wanted a space that emulated the style of old farm kitchens.

SOLUTION

- Load the kitchen with culinary conveniences, including a six-burner professional-grade stove, warming drawers, refrigerator drawers, and a butler's pantry that serves as a service kitchen or baking center.
- Combine 21st-century cooking luxuries with farmhouse-style elements including vaulted ceilings and furniturelike cabinetry painted barn red.

1: One corner of the kitchen—complete with a cutting board, refrigerator drawers, and nearby sink on the island—serves as a highly functional workstation.

2: A multitude of drawers on the outside of the island keeps linens handy.

3: Red-finished, rural-inspired cabinetry frames the professional-grade stove that boasts six burners and warming drawers.

Contemporary Hospitality

Creating a crisp, contemporary kitchen aglow with heartwarming hospitality is nothing short of a modern miracle. Or so it seems in this kitchen, which balances contemporary styling with traditional warmth and coziness. Carefully chosen materials—mellow maple, brushed stainless steel, quartz surfacing, and a neutral-hue ceramic tile—transform the previously dark and dour space into a kitchen that caters to two avid cooks and warmly welcomes guests.

Removing a peninsula and ceiling-mount cabinets between the kitchen and breakfast area, adding new windows above each sink, and placing French doors in the breakfast bay allow more space-expanding daylight to flood the space. Now a 7-foot-long island topped with light-reflecting stainless steel separates the cooking and breakfast areas and creates space for side-by-side prepping. Open stainless-steel shelves on the working side of the island keep countertop clutter at bay, as does a tall storage unit nearby, which blends

1: Two sinks and two dishwashers flank the professional-grade range, providing plenty of room for two cooks to work side by side.

2: As part of the primary work zone, tall base cabinets and a high counter create a convenient landing spot for items removed from the waist-high microwave oven.

3: A stacked storage unit that pulls out corrals pots and lids on wire racks.

traditional wood with contemporary steel and glass and takes advantage of wall space without crowding the aisle around the island.

Two sinks and dishwashers further facilitate two cooks, as do the massive professional-grade range, exhaust hood, and dual ovens along one wall. The pale maple cabinets appear to "float" on a shiny ribbon of stainless steel, and open stainless-steel shelves above the counter in a corner imply abundant spaciousness.

S I T U A T I O N

- The former kitchen design was so minimalist that the room felt cold and uninviting.
- To truly accommodate two cooks, the kitchen required more footage than previously allotted.

S O L U T I O N

- Pair the warmth of maple cabinetry with the stark lines and cool tones of stainless-steel appliances.

- Steal 2 feet from a nearby room to yield enough space for dual sinks, a dishwasher, and a professional-grade range on an outside wall.

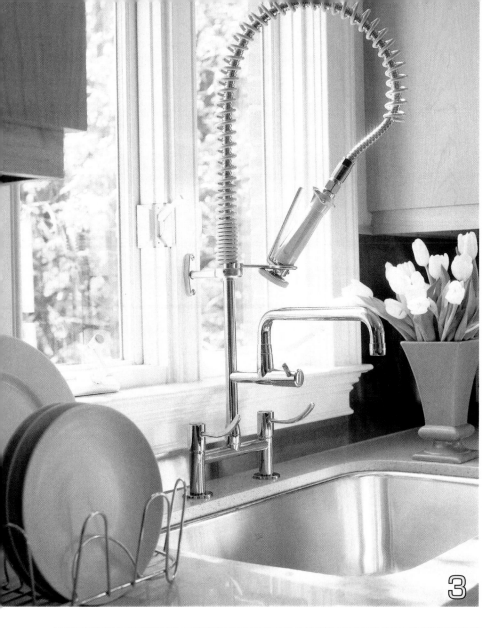

1: An auxiliary dishwasher, a cleanup sink, and a new window replaced a rarely used desk in the breakfast area.

2: Open shelves on the working side of the island keep everyday items at hand. The island base includes discreet electrical outlets for small appliances that are stored away when not in use.

3: An extra-deep cleanup sink and restaurant-inspired faucet with a flexible sprayer ensure even big pots get cleaned.

4: The unencumbered beauty of the quartz-surface countertop, pale maple cabinets, and stainless-steel backsplash is enhanced by the fact that they're easy to clean.

5: Traditional wood and contemporary steel and glass unite in the tall storage unit, which looks like an ultramodern armoire.

History Lessons

Inspired by the architecture of Colonial structures in historic Williamsburg, Virginia, this brand-new kitchen re-creates the best of the past. The kitchen's historical character comes from its distressed pine cabinets that change heights, depths, and styles for visual variety. Cloaking new amenities in old looks furthers the era-appropriate styling—the refrigerator and dishwasher wear panels that match the cabinets. The pine planks and crown molding blend the stainless-steel ventilation hood above the professional-grade range with the rest of the room. The island serves as the primary work surface and distinguishes the dining and cooking areas. It boasts a red finish and black granite countertop that contrasts with the speckled granite on top of the perimeter cabinets. With the addition of a brick-faced hearth, the kitchen warmly celebrates the history of Colonial-era keeping rooms.

SITUATION

- The brand-new kitchen needed to exude old-fashioned, inviting Colonial style.
- Period-appropriate design dictated the inclusion of a hearth.

SOLUTION

- Mix wood finishes and cabinet sizes to suggest an unfitted kitchen assembled over time.
- Include a rustic fireplace made from salvaged lumber and handmade bricks.

1

1: The mix of wood finishes and cabinet sizes suggests the kitchen's pine cabinets and island were brought in over time even though they are actually brand-new built-in pieces.

2: The Colonial-red finish of the island makes it a visual as well as functional room divider. The pine-paneled refrigerator to the left resembles an antique armoire.

3: The rustic fireplace warms the kitchen and dining area even when there's no fire in it. The arched cubby to the right is a working bread oven.

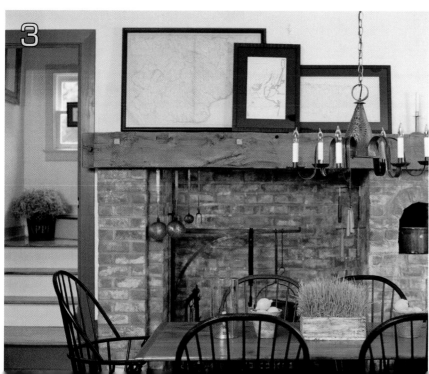

Finessing the Floor Plan

Subtly tweaking a seemingly inflexible floor plan and replacing old cabinets helps make the most of every inch of this tiny high-rise kitchen. Narrowing a doorway to the dining room by a mere 2 inches allows for a foot of countertop on either side of the cooktop and placement of the stacked oven and microwave oven on the same wall. On another wall, a narrow pantry cabinet pairs with a new refrigerator for easily accessible food storage. Replacing an old electric-coil cooktop with a smooth ceramic glass unit saves inches. This way the cooktop becomes additional counter space when not in use. Most spectacular of all, a curved granite-top table positioned over an immovable radiator provides breathtaking views and lends extra work space.

SITUATION

- An inflexible floor plan meant expansion wasn't an option.
- Moving from a house with a large kitchen to a condominium with a small one meant sacrificing storage space.
- The unattractive 30-year-old cabinetry needed an update.

SOLUTION

- Cluster appliances—such as a cooktop and stacked wall oven and microwave oven—along one wall to maximize available space.
- Sneak in storage options, such as a towering combination wine rack and bookcase, on a previously wasted wall.
- Replace the cabinetry with storage-intensive fitted maple models outfitted with contemporary hardware.

1: The curved granite-top table that spans the window provides a perch for taking in stunning views of San Francisco and the Golden Gate Bridge.

2: Below the electric cooktop, wide, deep drawers store pots and pans.

3: Translucent glass panels and slender pulls enhance the sleek, fitted maple cabinetry.

4: Bifold doors above the sink can remain open for cooking and cleanup convenience.

Air Supply

A modest-size kitchen gains a boost with an L-shape layout that opens to a sunny courtyard. Dutch doors custom-fit with glass panels and a ceiling topped with architecturally boxed ceiling soffits allow light and breezes to stream through the space. Mixing cool metal and warm wood tones helps anchor the open-air feel; acid-etched concrete on the floor lends another earthy note. In keeping with the contemporary look, cabinetry finished in a deep-gray laminate with wood-veneer accents is accompanied by tubular stainless-steel pulls. The stacked wall oven and microwave oven fit neatly in a pantry wall next to an appliance niche. Smart details, including sized-to-fit storage, ensure the space remains tidy yet airy.

SITUATION

- The tiny 12×21-foot kitchen offered little storage space.
- Cutting boards took up precious counterspace.

SOLUTION

- Install European modular cabinetry and sized-to-fit storage.
- Raise two sections of solid-surfacing to serve as built-in cutting boards.

1: Glass-panel Dutch entry doors offer easy access to an outdoor dining court and allow gentle breezes into the kitchen. Neutral expanses, such as the stainless-steel backsplash and refrigerator, help the space look uncluttered.

2: The kitchen offers two sunny spots for casual dining—at the raised island bar and at a cozy table. Both receive light from ample windows and the glass-insert Dutch doors. The countertops and table are topped with white solid-surfacing with flat edges.

3: Ample storage space is generated in the kitchen through a well-designed mix of open and closed cabinetry. A long bar spanning the cooktop backsplash provides easy access to hanging utensils and spices.

Asian Influence

A kitchen rooted in the natural simplicity of Asian heritage is only fitting for a homeowner who grew up in Japan. The 15×20-foot room's centerpiece is a sizable and distinctively shaped island. It's designed to serve as a command post, a family dining area, and a perch for enjoying views from the huge picture window centered along the closed end of the J-shape layout. The maple cabinetry boasts simple lines and minimal decorative details to set a contemporary tone. Bronze tiles create a backsplash with Asian flavor without overwhelming the already bright kitchen. Paired with granite countertops, the maple cabinets and backsplash tiles succeed in creating a warm yet contemporary translation of Asian style in this Midwestern home.

SITUATION

- A new kitchen required room for an island and a picture window to take advantage of views.
- The homeowner wanted to use influences from her home country of Japan in the kitchen design.

SOLUTION

- Create a J-shape layout that places the island in the center of the room and the picture window along the closed end of the J.
- Select clean-lined cabinetry, granite countertops, and bronze metal backsplash tiles for a contemporary Asian look.

1: A prep sink at the island creates the perfect workstation for rinsing produce or filling pots headed for the cooktop.

2: A custom island allows the whole family to sit together for casual meals and enjoy the views through the picture window. Clean-lined cabinets with long, slender pulls complement the stainless-steel appliances.

3: The windows above the main sink allow a bird's-eye view of the neighborhood. A double-bowl sink and set of dishwasher drawers ease cleanup.

House Blend

Much as a coffee shop offers a respite from a hectic world, this cozy kitchen in an 1880s Italianate home exudes warmth and comfort. The effort to transform the home from chopped-up rental units back to its single-family status began in the kitchen, where the long-grain pine floors and oversize wood-frame windows were refinished. A revamped work triangle places appliances on either side of a corner sink, and a two-tier island with a second sink and butcher-block top adds more prep space. In a nod to the past, the upper kitchen cabinets feature beading and recessed center panels, while the smooth styling of the lower ones meshes with the stainless-steel elements. An original exposed brick wall forms the backdrop for a sitting area across from the kitchen, completing the coffeehouse appeal.

1: Next to the kitchen, a sitting room with an exposed brick wall, old-fashioned windows, and long-grain pine floors exudes warmth and charm.

2: Space for circulating is essential in a compact kitchen. Here guests can gather at the end of the center island or pull up a stool next to it. The frosted-glass-front cabinet at the end of the island offers additional storage for everyday dishes.

3: A retractable cutting board fits perfectly inside a knife drawer.

Nothing to Hide

A farmhouse kitchen should be at the heart of daily family life, but this rural home's dark, hemmed-in cooking space was isolated from family living areas and provided nowhere to eat. To remedy this, the kitchen was rebuilt as part of a large space that includes a family room and eating area. The U-shape core, which is grounded by two wooden structural posts, takes center stage. Two-way upper cabinets on the side by the family room provide a curtain of sorts for cooking productions. Posts and pine cabinets tie the kitchen to the home's wooded site, while the surrounding pale green walls and white trim keep the mood bright and natural.

SITUATION

- A small L-shape corner kitchen didn't appeal to a family who enjoys cooking and entertaining.
- The kitchen, situated in the middle of a living area, looked as if it were floating in space.

SOLUTION

- Combine a new U-shape kitchen with other family areas for a large, inviting living space.
- Use structural posts to ground the kitchen and tie the area to the rest of the home's wooden elements.

1: The base of the work core serves as a divider between the kitchen and family room. Upper cabinets are accessible from both sides, while a long, curved ledge is a natural serving area. The lower cabinets conceal a TV that's positioned for family-room viewing.

2: A modest bump-out makes room for an eating area along one side of the work core. The area takes advantage of light and views at the back of the house.

3: Moving the kitchen's work core from a dark corner to the middle of reconfigured family living space gives the homeowners' passion for cooking greater prominence and a brighter setting. Posts and upper cabinets partially enclose the U-shape area without isolating it.

4: The sink's granite countertop and old-look faucet are fitting choices for a late-1800s farmhouse. Views from the sink include the deck and outdoors beyond.

Narrow Passage

Galley kitchens are by nature narrow spaces. But this kitchen, in an 1830 Greek Revival home, was more restricted than most. Working within the space's original footprint, the homeowners managed to enlarge the area by annexing a pantry on one side and creating a sitting room from two small rooms on the other. Although the kitchen's decor is not a strict interpretation of the period, the enlarged space blends traditional custom cabinets and trim with industrial stainless-steel countertops and appliances and a rustic reclaimed floor to create timeless style.

SITUATION

- Worn laminate countertops and a vinyl floor made the galley kitchen seem dated and small.
- The old, white appliances didn't fit with the kitchen's proposed new style.
- Recessed lighting looked incongruous with a historic house.

SOLUTION

- Update the space using reclaimed stone for the floor and stainless steel for the countertops.
- Splurge on stainless-steel appliances, including two refrigerator drawers, two wall ovens, and a warming drawer.
- Install reproduction wrought-iron chandeliers to evenly distribute light.

1. To maximize storage space, pots and pans hang on a wall rack. The reclaimed stone on the floor was laid out before sealing to ensure the color and sizes were random.
2. Roll-out spice racks below the cooktop mean seasonings are at the cook's fingertips.
3. This galley kitchen blends traditional and industrial elements—including stainless-steel countertops, reproduction wrought-iron chandeliers, and a reclaimed stone floor.

3

Rooms Around the Kitchen

If you're thinking about remodeling an existing kitchen or building a new one, it's a perfect time to evaluate the rooms and areas that surround the traditional kitchen work core.

If your kitchen serves as your home's most-used entry, the addition or reworking of a mudroom—perhaps one that accommodates a laundry—could help ease kitchen mess and congestion.

Is the problem a lack of storage? Before you tear out a bank of windows to install floor-to-ceiling cabinets, consider whether a separate pantry might make more sense. No longer dark, stuffy little rooms that hide nonperishables, pantries have become practical and attractive kitchen storage and workspaces with amenities including refrigerators and second dishwashers.

Are you sick of sweeping the kitchen table free of bills and papers before every meal, or do you need a place for the kids to use the computer while you monitor their Internet surfing? A kitchen office might be just what you need. Locate your kitchen command center on the perimeter of the kitchen, away from the main work triangle. If you need extra storage space, make room for cubbyholes or deep drawers, which provide convenient spots to stash the kids' schoolbooks and backpacks.

Check out these ideas for creating the perfect mudroom, laundry, pantry, or kitchen command center near your kitchen work core.

1: This pantry's open storage demands order as well as style, which is achieved through the use of baskets, antique pitchers and bowls, and the antique coffee tin mounted on the wall.

2: A lovely laundry room repeats the kitchen cabinetry, backsplash, and apron-front sink found in the adjacent Colonial kitchen for a cohesive look. The front-loading washer and dryer are hidden behind the lower cabinet doors.

3: This easy-to-create mudroom consists of a series of hooks hung along a wall separating the entry from the dining room. Family members can leave messages for one another on the rectangular chalkboard next to the coats and boots.

1: Like the rest of the kitchen, this office area is warm, bright, and functional. A long granite desktop provides room for a computer, and the shelves above hold collectibles and books.

2: To blend with its modern kitchen, this pantry features dark, flat-front cabinets with sandblasted glass set in aluminum. The semitransparent glass hints at what's stored in the cabinets without distracting from the rest of the kitchen.

3: With glass-front cabinets and decorative tile, this butler's pantry complements the kitchen's cottage look. Equipped with a sink, microwave oven, countertop appliances, and dinnerware storage, the pantry serves as an auxiliary food-prep center.

Find Your Style

1

The foundation of every kitchen is essentially the same: cabinetry, appliances, countertops, backsplash, and flooring. It's the detailing that gives each kitchen a unique look. Cabinetry materials and finishes, door styling, colors, textures, handles and pulls, light fixtures, and appliance appearance and location all play a role in the look of your kitchen.

Contrary to what you may think, style does not have to come with a high price tag. Lower-price stock cabinets are available in a wide range of finishes and styles. Even if you crave a professional-look kitchen on a modest budget, beefy stainless-steel appliances once found only in high-end spaces are now available for more modest funds; of course you won't get all of the features found in top-of-the-line products, but you can have the style.

A successfully remodeled or new kitchen should be a combination of function and style. In fact, the impetus for the majority of kitchen projects is dissatisfaction with what looks like a dated room. It's during the planning stages that homeowners—often with the help of designers, architects, or contractors—realize how much they can improve the function, efficiency, and work flow of the kitchen. So take a style tour of a few of the many options available.

Traditional kitchens exude a warm, rich feeling thanks to wood cabinets—often cherry or oak finished in medium to darker stains. As the name suggests,

1: Sleek stainless-steel pulls, tall stainless legs on the island, and metal and decorative-glass-panel doors in the upper wall cabinets offer a contemporary feel, illustrating that modern styling can feel at home in an otherwise traditional-style space.

2: Richly stained wood cabinetry featuring raised-panel doors sets the tone for this traditional kitchen. The dramatic stove and vent hood surrounded by a paneled mantel serves as the focal point of the room.

2

1

2

traditional kitchens typically stand the test of time and don't look dated as quickly as other designs. Raised-panel cabinet doors, turned legs, and bun feet on tables, cabinets, islands, and peninsulas contribute to a furniture-style look. Traditional style, especially in recent interpretations, needn't be fussy. It can offer a clean aesthetic, but with a softer, warmer side than most contemporary kitchens.

Contemporary kitchen designs include the gleaming, stainless-steel and concrete kitchens that once defined this category. As with any style, over time the definition of contemporary style has expanded to include fun, bright colors, and more open floor plans than other styles. Cabinet details include textured-glass door panels and frameless construction.

Vintage kitchens often re-create or maintain a style appropriate to the era of the house. It's also possible to design a vintage-look kitchen in a newer house simply because you want to establish a sense of history in the midst of a new suburb. Period details are available in new fixtures, appliances, and other products designed to look old but with modern functions, and in salvaged materials.

Global design is becoming a more significant style influence. Often these kitchens make a very personal statement because the design is sparked by childhood memories of a distant home or treasured finds collected in world travels. Asian styling—with soothing, often minimalist lines, natural colors and materials, and textures pleasing to the touch—is also popular as more

homeowners strive to create a serene oasis at home to escape the cares of the day.

Eclectic styling recognizes that often the most successful designs are a pleasing combination of the things you like best. This approach encourages a mix of materials and styles. When done right, the outcome is not a hodgepodge of mismatched items, but a comfortable, inviting space.

1: Details including bin pulls, nickel-finish fixtures, and beaded-board cabinet door insets are essential in this vintage kitchen.

2: Traditional elements from Spanish, French, and Italian villas combine in this space dominated by cream-color concrete counters, red cedar cabinet doors, and a weathered range hood.

3: Craftsman-style cabinetry partners with a contemporary stainless-steel range and geometric stove vent in this eclectic-style kitchen.

Refreshing your kitchen doesn't mean breaking the bank. If your kitchen feels a bit worn and dreary, but has enough space for your needs and a good layout, take note. The kitchens in this section prove that some relatively quick-and-easy changes can have major impact. Packed with real-life applications of clever ideas, this chapter will help you create a kitchen with vibrance and vitality—even on a budget.

refresh

Fashion-Forward Flashback

How do you combine old and new for a fresh look that's neither slavishly retro nor jarringly contemporary? In this 1950s kitchen, it involves never losing sight of the space's mid-century roots. After a coat of fresh paint and the addition of new reeded-glass sliding doors, the original metal cabinets become the focal point. A lively ceramic tile backsplash, uplights in the shortened soffits, and sleek stainless-steel appliances add a modern touch. Trading dowdy yellow laminate and garish orange vinyl for gleaming granite counters and maple flooring lends a timeless element. The light wood of the flooring is repeated in a chunky windowsill and attractive wall storage.

SITUATION

- Homeowners liked the period details of their 1950s home, but worn elements in the kitchen needed to be refreshed.
- The original cabinets had potential, but the dark brown paint and chipped panels needed some work.
- Proposed new elements would need to mix seamlessly with the old.

SOLUTION

- Update, rather than replace, the original cabinets.
- Paint the cabinets buttercup yellow and seafoam green and replace the upper cabinets' panels with glass doors.
- Design the new custom storage to links to the existing cabinets through hardware and clean lines.

1: An expanse of custom storage includes a convenient parking spot for a rolling butcher-block table.

2: The floor-to-ceiling maple wall unit harmonizes with new wood flooring.

3: The dark brown metal doors on the original bottom cabinets were repainted buttercup yellow and seafoam green. For the upper cabinets, the original panels were replaced with pristine reeded-glass sliding doors.

1

Face-Saving Moves

The room-by-room remodel of this 1926 Tudor-style home progressed smoothly until it reached the kitchen, where the outdated cupboards detracted from the house's character and Craftsman-style woodwork. Instead of being relegated to the trash, however, the laminate cabinets received new door and drawer fronts for a budget-smart facelift. New stainless-steel countertops and matching stainless-steel appliances offset the dark wood. Halogen lighting in the ceiling and under the upper cabinets further illuminates the space. To finish the room, tumbled-marble mosaic tile with a radiant-heat system underneath creates a striking flooring surface.

SITUATION

- The 1980s laminate cabinets didn't suit the Tudor-style house.
- Too much wood made the kitchen seem dark and drab.
- Undercabinet hockey-puck-shape fixtures protruded too far beneath the cabinets.

SOLUTION

- Cover the cabinets with new oak-veneer plywood and oak strips to echo the spirit of the woodwork throughout the house.
- Counterbalance the dark with the gleam of stainless-steel countertops and appliances.
- Install 2-inch-wide aluminum angle strips as "skirts" on the bottom of the upper cabinets to hide the light fixtures.

1: The refrigerator next to the stainless-steel stove and microwave oven blends with the new cabinet doors.

2: A vintage telephone hangs above a nifty flip-down shelf in a spot once occupied by a drop-down ironing board.

3: Rather than completely replacing the cabinetry, new door and drawer faces were built onto the existing cabinet frames.

1

Bungalow Basics

Considering the rest of the 1920s Spanish-style bungalow was gutted and completely remodeled, it was surprising that its kitchen required only a cosmetic makeover. With a limited budget and no room to work outside the home's original footprint, the homeowner chose to create a loftlike floor plan. Consistent style throughout is key, particularly because the open layout means guests entering the front door catch a glimpse of the kitchen at the back of the home. New French doors in the kitchen match those located at the front entry. To fit with the abundant maple used throughout the home, the original cabinetry was refaced with a maple veneer. Compensating for a lack of storage and counter space in the compact kitchen, the high-top table serves as a peninsula and an open storage unit—illustrating the artful way this space combines simple style and function.

1: By refacing the cabinetry with maple veneer and keeping the original slate countertop, the homeowner was able to freshen up this compact kitchen for less.

2: The dining room provides views into the kitchen and serves as a pass-through between the living area and cooking space.

3: The wheels attached to the high-top kitchen table, which also serves as a peninsula, glide smoothly over the new metallic-green flooring.

4: Like the kitchen table, a stainless-steel rack on wheels serves as movable storage.

1

Unconventional Accents

With creative collecting and a slew of cosmetic changes, even a tiny Texas cottage kitchen exudes an unusual take on Craftsman style. The wide-open kitchen just off the living room boasts plenty of cabinets, a 30-inch professional-grade range, and a built-in wine cooler in the island. For textural variety, the countertops and backsplash are covered in terra-cotta tile a shade similar to the hammered copper covering the ventilation hood above the range. Beaded-board panels adorn the sides of the custom island, which is topped with maple from a worktable more than 30 years old. Furthering the history of the room, an Arts and Crafts pottery collection fills a hutch along one wall, and the hanging lights that illuminate the space were saved from an old country bank.

- The ventilation hood was little more than an unsightly plywood box.
- Without color, the abundant cabinetry bordered on boring.

- Cover the hood with textured copper sheeting and upholstery tacks.
- Paint the cabinets with a custom-mixed green-gray hue. Add a terra-cotta tile backsplash to offset the cabinets.

1: The refrigerator appears built-in thanks to the green cabinets that surround it. The cabinets hide ductwork and a sound system.
2: The tiled countertops and backsplashes coordinate with the color of the hand-hammered copper that covers the ventilation hood.
3: The copper sink and fixtures lend additional old-world flair.

Refresher Course

With too much brown and too little color, this small kitchen suffered from a bland decorating diet until a couple of gallons of paint created a kitchen full of flavor. Although the kitchen boasted an open layout and new white appliances, it suffered from a dreary color scheme. To remedy the situation, the homeowner painted the cabinets a tomato-inspired bright red, and covered random tile squares along the white backsplash with black paint. New laminate countertops, track lighting, and storage shelves add further functionality and style to the space. An inexpensive black and white checkerboard vinyl floor complements the backsplash to finish the look.

SITUATION

- With time and money constraints, the homeowner needed a quick kitchen fix.
- The sage green walls didn't match the dark oak cabinets.
- The plain white tile backsplash needed a boost.

SOLUTION

- Tackle one thing at a time to create a vintage-style kitchen with a bright personality for less than $1,200.
- Paint the cabinets a bright red and adorn them with jewel-like knobs.
- Tape off random tile squares and cover them with black paint.

1: The seven-shelf storage cabinet in the corner by the table was constructed from inexpensive wood and painted green to match the walls. Baskets provide ample storage.

2: The jewel-like green knobs would have been too expensive to use on every cabinet, so they adorn only the upper units.

3: The new black and white vinyl tiles were installed on top of the old linoleum to match the black squares painted on the white tile backsplash.

3

A Black-Tie Affair

Successfully designing a tuxedo kitchen on a business-casual budget is possible as long as you follow the mantra, "If it's paid for, make it work." To ensure consistency among the appliances, a black panel covers the almond door of the dishwasher, and a new glass cooktop and microwave oven replace the old ones. To blend the existing cabinetry with the appliances, graphite-color paint was used on the stained wood. Whitewashed wood floors and light-color ceramic tile countertops and backsplashes balance the dark elements. Recessed ceiling cans and undercabinet lighting brighten the room artificially, while a wall of glass block and a large window above the sink add natural light.

SITUATION

- Ho-hum builder cabinets and worn laminate flooring made this kitchen a yawn.
- Remodeling on a budget meant all new appliances were out of the question.
- A poorly designed preparation island took up much-needed space.

SOLUTION

- Cover the stained cabinets with graphite-color paint and install new, light-color wood flooring.
- Hold on to appliances that match the decor and are still in good condition; replace or modify those that don't match or are too old.
- Replace the original island with one that includes seating and storage.

1: Glass block replaced a sliding glass door on an exterior wall, providing privacy while ensuring the kitchen is filled with abundant light.
2: The warm tones of the tile counters and whitewashed wood floors balance the dark cabinetry and appliances.

Priceless Improvements

Savvy do-it-yourself ideas turn a 1970s-style kitchen into a graceful, modern room without a hefty price tag. Instead of costly major construction to improve the layout, the kitchen underwent a minor structural change that yielded big results. Because new cabinetry was too expensive, the original cabinet doors were revamped with grass-cloth wallpaper and taupe paint. The Mexican limestone tiles on the countertops, backsplashes, and floors are an affordable alternative to European limestone, and the rough plaster-finish walls and ceiling create warmth and character. Well-chosen indulgences—a granite farmhouse-style sink and the butcher-block island—complete the serious style for less.

SITUATION

- Moving walls would have been too costly, but the layout needed help.
- The dated kitchen needed a facelift but refacing or replacing the cabinets wasn't an option.
- The budget didn't allow for desired European limestone slab countertops.

SOLUTION

- Open a pass-through between the sink and dining room to connect the two spaces visually.
- Cover the cabinet doors with grass-cloth wallpaper, frame them with molding, and paint the cabinetry taupe.
- Install Mexican limestone tiles on the countertops, backsplashes, and floors as an attractive, affordable alternative.

1: The butcher-block island, another focal point, was constructed from an antique butcher block fitted on a mesquite base.

2: Instead of refacing or replacing the cabinets, the homeowners chose to cover the existing cupboards with grass cloth.

Cosmetic Cures

This dated kitchen's update involved cooking up some creative ideas for making do on a budget without settling for stale. First to go was the old linoleum floor, which was replaced with 12-inch-square tiles from a local home center. The cabinet doors, like the linoleum, couldn't be salvaged. Instead, new, clean-lined doors constructed with lumberyard wood and simple modern pulls saved money while infusing the kitchen with fresh attitude. Two shades of green paint topped with hand-painted images of bowls, cups, and plates add a personal touch. Replacing the dated countertops and white tile backsplash wasn't in the budget—instead, counters gleam with new stainless-steel caps, and glass mosaic tiles accent select spots along the backsplash. The result is a bright, cheery kitchen that doesn't break the bank.

SITUATION

- The dull, yellow-cream kitchen lacked inspiration.
- Replacing the dated countertops and tile backsplash wasn't in the budget.
- In a small kitchen, countertop space was too crowded.

SOLUTION

- Personalize the room by painting the cabinets green and adding hand-drawn designs.
- Cook up creative ideas—including adding glass mosaic tile accents and capping the countertop with stainless steel.
- Use creative options such as a suspended shelf to house the microwave above the stove and off the countertops.

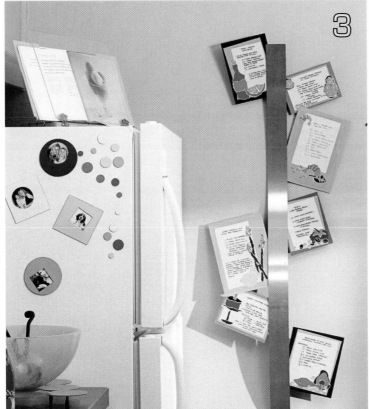

1: Budget-wise additions, such as the stainless-steel caps that cover the existing countertops, enhance the kitchen.

2: The colors in the specialty Roman shade found above the window match those in the glass backsplash inset tiles.

3: A metal holder displays often-used recipes within reach.

4: Colorful glass tiles draw attention away from the dated, gold-flecked backsplash.

Industrial Finish

In today's kitchens, the industrial gleam of stainless steel packs a contemporary punch, but back in the 1950s it possessed an almost space-age look. Combining striking colors and diner-era nostalgia, one interior designer welded industrial and retro elements to create this riveting kitchen that's a throwback to the Eisenhower era.

Rather than tossing the two-year-old soft white cabinets, the designer chose to do away with the toe-the-line traditional style by spraying the surfaces with a glossy automobile lacquer and outfitting them with slender stainless-steel pulls. This left room in the budget to add a built-in buffet in the former breakfast area and revamp the old island with smooth, contemporary-style drawers and stainless-steel legs.

The island is topped with its original granite, and the same granite is found in the butler's pantry-style area opposite the island. Stainless-steel door frames ensure that side of the kitchen relates to the stainless steel in the cooking area. Diamond-pattern wire embedded in the glass inserts in the cabinet doors (see next page) ties into the pattern of the quilted stainless-steel backsplash located throughout the room.

Strategic bursts of bright red and yellow pop out against the mostly neutral surfaces. Parts of the upper cabinets are painted a racy red, as are the base units. The industrial-look fixture above the island features shocking yellow shades. The result is a kitchen that proves 50's touches and state-of-the-art can play, creating a nostalgic touch in a modern kitchen.

High-gloss gray automobile lacquer combines with stainless steel and strategic bursts of bright red and yellow to infuse the kitchen with industrial edginess and '50s style.

SITUATION

- Nearly-new, soft white cabinets were traditional in style while the homeowner preferred a retro-industrial look.
- A proposed plan for using only gray and stainless steel would have made an industrial kitchen boring.
- A large collection of china and glassware required ample storage.

SOLUTION

- Apply glossy automobile lacquer for a factory finish.
- Add splashes of bright red and yellow to energize the neutral surfaces. Install a quilted stainless-steel backsplash and valance.
- Build a new buffet into an old breakfast area, pack the workspace with plenty of upper and lower cabinetry, and load the island with drawers.

1: The upper cabinets in the butler's pantry feature new doors made of stainless steel, industrial glass, and embedded wire.

2: An area opposite the island functions as an in-kitchen butler's pantry. Red appears in the colorful chairs, rug, and cabinets.

3: Low-profile appliances, including an undercabinet microwave oven and built-in refrigerator with cabinetry-matching panels, blend with industrial-look cabinetry.

Country and Funky

Newly constructed homes are often built for mass appeal—not serious style. Yet this kitchen teems with character while saving money thanks to clever updates and plenty of color. A deep red crackle finish covers the walls. The cabinets were sanded, primed, painted, sealed again, and glazed with sunny yellow results. To get big bang for the decorating dollar, white tile replaces the beige laminate countertop. Layers of detail—including a vintage dairy sign above the stove, red-check tea towels on the windows, and wrought-iron and black hardware—complete the look.

SITUATION

- The freshly built kitchen lacked style.
- Clean, unmarred standard-fare oak cabinets and white walls were boring.
- New flooring would have been an expensive addition on top of the other improvements.

SOLUTION

- Create the look of a custom kitchen that's packed with personal touches and brimming with nostalgic warmth.
- Repaint the cabinets a cheery yellow and cover the walls in a deep red crackle finish.
- Wait until later to replace the faux-stone vinyl floor, which doesn't detract from the new look.

1: A cadre of red-edge enamelware lids hangs above the windows in the dining area. Tea towels were sewn together to create the roller shades.

2: A vintage dairy sign unifies the kitchen's elements and provides a funky focal point above the stove.

3: Continuing the country-meets-contemporary attitude, a mini coffee bar combines a high-tech stainless-steel espresso maker and retro-style bean grinder with vintage dishes and linens.

Stock Options

Dinnertime revolved around eating out until this once-dated kitchen received a much-needed update. In their quest for light, storage options, and an eating area, the homeowners created a fresh, affordable new look with stock materials. The floor plan fix involved rearranging the appliances and adding an eat-in area that anchors one end of the galley-style space. At the other end, a breakfast bar separates the living room and kitchen. In between, the old cupboards were replaced with clean-lined cabinets in the same blond tone as the new laminate flooring. Now cooking and eating in are the norm, rather than the exception.

SITUATION

- A dated 1960s color scheme needed a fresh look.
- An ill-conceived layout placed the refrigerator right next to the stove, creating an awkward work area.
- No space for eating at home sent the homeowners out to eat more than they preferred.

SOLUTION

- Use the neutral colors of maple cabinets, stainless-steel appliances, dark gray countertops, and white tile for a subdued, modern look.

- Rearrange the appliances to create a more traditional work triangle.
- Include a built-in bench, table, and chairs to make dining in easy.

1: Now that the kitchen is open to the living room, guests can sit at the breakfast bar and chat with a cook working at the stove.

2: The palm-tree print pillows and black ticking-covered cushion on the bench add splashes of low-commitment color to the otherwise subdued kitchen.

3: Minimal upper cabinets with glass inserts, an attention-grabbing faucet, and a subway tile backsplash bring interest to an otherwise plain wall.

4: Storage compartments hold toys and seldom-used kitchen items beneath the built-in bench.

Curing the Condominium

Discussion of penthouse condos typically brings to mind tall, concrete buildings filled with luxury. This neglected penthouse, however, was located in a low, squat building that did little to live up to its lofty moniker. Instead of gutting the space, the homeowners chose to focus on filling the Eastern Seaboard condo with Arts and Crafts style. In the kitchen, this meant the original, sturdy oak cabinets stayed, but the upper ones were painted white, fitted with wire inserts, and raised to make the beaded-board wainscoting backsplash taller. A new linoleum floor and the addition of a pass-through to the dining area complete the transition from ill-fitting kitchen to memorable condo cookspace.

SITUATION

- The awkward penthouse condo kitchen was too cramped.
- Storage space was limited because the kitchen was so narrow.

SOLUTION

- Rework the kitchen to make it seem bigger by raising the upper cabinets, removing the doors between the kitchen and living areas, and creating a new pass-through to the dining table.
- Build two floor-to-ceiling pantries to flank the pass-through to the living room.

1: A portion of the wall between the kitchen and dining table was carved out and trimmed with the same type of molding used elsewhere in the house. The new pass-through provides easy access to the dining table.

2: Cooking utensils hang from a stainless-steel rail mounted to the cabinets above the sink.

3: The rabbit-hutch wire used for the inside panels of the upper cabinet doors adds splashes of silver that meld with the mellow look of the new enamel paint. The new linoleum floor is laid on the diagonal to make the tight room seem larger.

3

Fresh Hues

1

This spacious 21×29-foot kitchen had an efficient island layout, big windows, and plentiful storage, including a butler's pantry. With an arctic expanse of white tile, white cabinetry, and icy blue accents, however, the space was the antithesis of color-confident style. The kitchen didn't require a remodel—it needed to be thawed out.

Now the walls are painted a butter-yellow hue that carries over to the cabinets in the pass-through butler's pantry. The work core pairs denim-blue base cabinets with upper cabinets in a pale blue inspired by a well-worn chambray shirt. For even more variety, the island is painted a vibrant green with a green-gold glaze. Beyond the lively color, distressed finishes give the standard cabinets a more custom look. Three countertop surfaces differentiate work spaces—white ceramic tile adorns the cook's corner, Jerusalem stone covers the island, and maple butcher-block tops the peninsula.

SITUATION

- This kitchen possessed great bones but a cold heart with white cabinetry and icy blue accents.
- Too much white ceramic tile meant a bland expanse of countertop.

SOLUTION

- Change the colors and generate warmth with welcoming blues, yellows, and greens on the cabinetry and walls.
- Cover the island top with Jerusalem stone, the peninsula with butcher block, and the countertop edging with natural wood trim for variety.

1: Although the kitchen's layout remained the same, the addition of shades of denim blue, green, and yellow dramatically changed the character of the space.

2: A desk in the kitchen features display space for pieces of spongeware and boasts the same distressed finish and butcher-block top used throughout the space.

3: The cook's corner situated between the refrigerator and range creates space for food prep away from island traffic.

One Kitchen Three Ways

No matter how well your kitchen functions, someday you may decide to rethink its look. Changing your kitchen's surface treatments—walls, floors, cabinet fronts and finishes, countertops, fixtures, hardware, lighting, and furnishings—facilitates amazing transformations, energizing the room's look without breaking your budget. Glean inspiration for your own kitchen revival from these three options, all of which have been applied to the same standard kitchen space.

CREATE YOUR OWN COTTAGE STYLE

Make smart choices to re-create this timeless look on a budget.

- Insert beaded-board panels in frameless stock upper cabinets.
- Cap a backsplash at 4 inches so both the countertop and backsplash can be cut from the same 36-inch-wide slab.
- Paint 6-inch-wide planks to complete the backsplash.
- Cover the entire floor with 12×12-inch porcelain tiles and forgo a custom border.
- Select white appliances—generally the least expensive appliance color—to match the white cabinetry.

STYLE 1: COTTAGE

Cottage style is all about living simply and comfortably. Personal collections are often showcased in baskets or on open shelving in this casual space. The tones are warm, and when color is introduced, it appears as muted brights such as ocean blue, buttery yellow, or seafoam green. Freestanding flea market finds, such as a weathered cabinet or old farm table, evoke memories of yesteryear. Typically more than one wood finish is integrated into the space, and even new furnishings echo the well-worn contours of nostalgic designs. Brushed metals—for cabinet hardware, light fixtures, and even the kitchen faucet—set off the look.

1: An ogee edge treatment—an S-shape profile—gives the island's solid-surfacing countertop a soft look.

2: In a nod to classic cottage style, a collection of bottles found at a flea market rest on a tiny shelf above the sink.

3: Tranquil colors and period detailing ensure a cottage kitchen is pretty without feeling cluttered. The new island's natural wood tone sets it apart from the white cabinetry, while the same countertop unifies the space.

STYLE 2: PATINA

The patina look offers a modern interpretation of two elegant kitchen styles—Old World and traditional—in warm, rich tones. The timeworn appeal involves layering textures for visual depth. In this case, glazed cabinetry pairs with wood flooring and tile countertops that look like natural stone. Little accents, such as a brushed-metal faucet and period door pulls, make a big statement. Flexible, freestanding pieces resemble furniture and serve as a counterpoint to built-in cabinetry. In this kitchen, minimal ornamentation lends a sophisticated edge to an otherwise traditional style.

CREATE YOUR OWN PATINA LOOK

Carefully choose where to splurge to keep your budget manageable.

• Mix and match stains on cabinets to create an expensive, custom look. Incorporate glass inserts into some of the cabinets to break up the solid expanse.
• Select prefinished engineered-wood flooring instead of springing for solid wood.
• Keep the cost of a tile countertop and backsplash low by running the backsplash tiles only one row deep and topping them with a ceramic chair rail.

1: Engineered-pine planks—formed in layers with a top layer of real pine—look like solid wood, lending an aged finish to the kitchen's floor.
2: The ceramic tile used on the countertop and backsplash looks like natural stone but costs much less.
3: The kitchen's warm character comes from its combination of colors and textures—including deep-red and charcoal-gray cabinetry, mottled ceramic tile, and distressed-look pine flooring.

CREATE YOUR OWN URBAN CHIC SPACE

This high-tech style can be achieved with some of the most budget-friendly materials available.

- Lay sheet vinyl flooring for an uninterrupted, neutral-color base.
- Select a laminate countertop instead of solid-surfacing.
- Go bold with a tumbled-slate tile backsplash, but use more economical materials on countertops and flooring to justify the splurge.
- Customize an expanse of stock maple cabinetry with frosted-glass inserts and stainless-steel hardware.

STYLE 3: URBAN CHIC

To achieve urban chic style in a modern kitchen, soften stark edges with organic forms and brighten a neutral palette with colorful accents. Inspired by the designs of the 1930s, '40s, and '50s, urban chic spaces are often pared down but not without personality. Favorite pieces, rather than an entire collection, are showcased. Simple lines, flat and featureless cabinet faces, and retro accents add interest. Mix matte and shiny finishes to fully capture the distinct style—don't forget to include stainless-steel, satin-chrome, and frosted-glass accents for a contemporary edge.

1: To dress up a simple line of stock maple cabinetry, add a beveled edge to an inexpensive laminate countertop.

2: A 4×4-inch slate-tile backsplash is the highlight of the space—it pulls together the warm maple tones of the cabinetry and the cooler gray countertops.

3: The urban chic kitchen combines a variety of finishes to create a sophisticated air. Bold red paint high up on the wall punches up the neutral palette.

IDEA FILE
Easy Updates

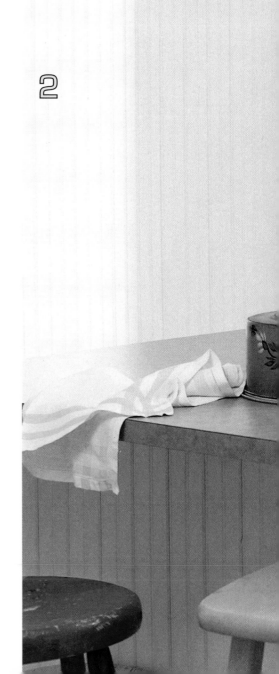

1: Undercabinet lights paired with recessed lights in the kitchen and table lights in the adjoining family room brighten both spaces without breaking the budget.

2: Crisp white cabinets perk up any kitchen. When cabinet structure is sound, a coat of paint can transform your kitchen into a cheery room like this one. Here white cabinetry and beaded-board paneling pair with pale green walls and accents for a fresh look.

When your kitchen needs a lift but major remodeling is out of the question, wake up the space with inexpensive changes that have a big impact. The results can be more vibrant and satisfying than you might have imagined—for little financial investment.

Paint. You can paint almost every surface—not just wood cabinets, but metal cabinets, wall paneling, floors, and even countertops and appliances—if you use special, highly durable epoxy finishes. Visit a paint supplier to see the products available for your specific needs. If you'd rather not do the job yourself, seek out companies that specialize in refinishing cabinets and countertops and ask for an estimate.

Develop an overall color scheme for the entire room rather than focusing on just one element. If the kitchen opens to other rooms—say a family room or dining room—look for color cues in those spaces. For additional color inspiration walk through your home and note the colors in your favorite items—clothing, artwork, furniture fabric, pottery, and home accessories can all provide ideas. Once you have a main color for the walls or the cabinets, select an accent color for a smaller element in the room. Pull in yet another accent color with table linens, window treatments, and accessories.

Lighting. Undercabinet lighting makes a dramatic difference in any kitchen. It's easy to mount either fluorescent or halogen fixtures beneath existing cabinets. Fluorescent light is diffused and it minimizes shadows; halogen fixtures create a bright white light that's perfect for task lighting, yet dimmable for mood lighting. If the only light source in the kitchen is a small, ceiling-mount fixture, consider having recessed or track lights installed to provide better overall light. Or replace the existing ceiling fixture with one that offers better, more attractive lighting. Visit a home center or lighting store to find individual lights and lighting strips to suit your needs.

1

Hardware. Replace, polish, or refinish your cabinet hardware. Think of it as jewelry for your kitchen—a relatively easy accessory to change. Choices are available in all styles and price ranges. Keep in mind, however, how many drawers and doors need to be outfitted. The gleaming $25 pull might seem like a bargain—until you purchase the 30 you need for the entire kitchen. A less expensive, similar style might be a better choice. Check local home centers and catalog and online retailers. If your new hardware choice is particularly eye-catching, consider using it sparingly for emphasis—for instance just on sink-side upper cabinets—supporting it with a simpler choice elsewhere in the kitchen.

Accessories. Kitchen accessories needn't be purely decorative. If you have a colorful set of dishes tucked away in a cabinet, consider display options that double as storage. Install open shelves on a vacant wall and stack dishes and cups in view. Or remove center panels from a couple of cabinets—the uppers on each side of the sink are good choices—and have them replaced with decorative glass. Contents stay tucked away yet in view. New window treatments and table linens are another simple way to bring a fresh look to your kitchen.

1: If you're painting cabinets a lively color—such as the green in this kitchen—install a few glass-panel doors to provide visual relief from the color. Pale walls and backsplashes also help ensure the color is pleasing rather than overwhelming.

2: Open shelves spanning two upper wall cabinets offer display space for decorative dishes and platters. The serving ware is easily accessed when needed and provides a welcome dash of color when on display.

3: New window valances are a simple way to update a kitchen. Choose fabric that will coordinate with the color scheme throughout the kitchen—and adjoining spaces if the kitchen is open. Valances are often the best choice above a sink where longer, full-length curtains would be exposed to splashing water.

One thing is certain. If you're looking to remodel, your kitchen requires more than new linoleum. What do you do? Identify what's most important—whether it's adding a wall or borrowing space from an adjacent room—to create the look and layout of your dreams. The finished product isn't going to materialize overnight, but the ideas in this chapter—a combination of moderate structural and cosmetic changes—can help you identify where you want to take your own remodel.

remodel

It's All in the Details

"Ugly brown everything" is not the ideal descriptor for a kitchen—or anything else in a house for that matter—but it can provide the impetus for change as it did here. Plagued by poor color choices and dated materials, this room was ripe for an overhaul.

But cosmetic changes alone wouldn't serve the needs of a busy family who loved to entertain—the end goal was a functional space with a fun personality. The project began with the removal of the wall formerly closing off the kitchen from the adjoining family room. Because this partition wall housed all the ductwork and electrical service for the second floor, two thick walls hiding the mechanicals were built where the two rooms meet. Green paint emphasizes the walls as an architectural feature rather than a structural necessity. The kitchen is further opened up by reconfiguring the island to allow for a connected table that seats six, replacing the former breakfast room that had been partitioned off by the old island.

1: An integral granite drainboard allows water to flow directly into the undermount sink.

2: The new pantry unit is thinner and shorter than the old unit, allowing more room for traffic flow and eliminating an unused top shelf. Thanks to a shelving system that adapts to contents as needed, the new unit provides just as much storage as the old pantry.

3: Attaching the table to the island allowed enough room for a table that seats six. Whimsical details such as the light fixture above the table make the kitchen fun and unique.

Contemporary overtones in the kitchen coordinate with the rest of the house, but unfitted cabinetry and varying wood tones provide the visual warmth the homeowners desire. A freestanding refrigerator with adjacent blue-painted pantry, wood legs on the island, and turned stainless-steel feet under the bar area all contribute to the unfitted look.

Details throughout add richness to the kitchen. Darker cherry accents on the upper cabinets, crown molding, and storage cubbies stand out against the light natural maple cabinets. Whimsical custom-made handles adorn the refrigerator. Though fanciful, most of the details are subtle so as to not overwhelm the space.

SITUATION

- Poor color choices and dated materials rendered this kitchen unappealing.
- The small kitchen, closed off from the living room, wasn't functional.

SOLUTION

- Use a variety of light maple and hickory woods with darker cherry design details to create a refreshing, contemporary space.
- Tear down the wall between the kitchen and family room. Connect the dining table to the island and eliminate the breakfast room.

1: A second convection oven is inconspicuously positioned in the island to prevent the appliances from dominating the room.

2: Glass shelves mounted to the window casing offer display space for collectibles without blocking the natural light and eliminate the need for a window treatment.

3: A wall was removed between the kitchen and family room. New hickory flooring further unites the two rooms. The varying tones of the floor relate to the various woods used elsewhere in the two rooms.

Enlightening a Classic

How do you make a modest-size kitchen serve a family of six without bumping out the walls? In this 13×20-foot kitchen, adding a peninsula to divide the space into multiple work areas with separate eating and cooking spaces was key. The peninsula provides essential additional counterspace while keeping the entire room open so the family can interact. Vintage-style, crisp-white cabinetry with beaded-board panels lightens the look of the once dark kitchen. Blue and white pottery serves as the inspiration for the color scheme, and as a decorative collection showcased in glass-fronted upper cabinets. A new set of windows replacing a formerly solid wall lets in natural light as well as views of the backyard, completing the cheery, family-friendly makeover.

SITUATION

- A small window with an unattractive view kept the kitchen in the dark.
- The space was too cramped for a family of six.
- Period elements were desirable but in disrepair.

SOLUTION

- Bring in more natural light and a view of the yard with a new bank of windows on another wall.
- Add counterspace to accommodate more cooks and include a peninsula to separate the eating and cooking areas.
- Use existing architectural features as the model for re-creating vintage style.

1: A new peninsula offers much-needed additional counterspace and divides the kitchen into separate cooking and eating areas. The new windows above the sink provide views of the backyard and let light brighten the room.

2: Blue paint inside the pantry cabinet doors enhances the collection of china that inspired the color palette for the kitchen.

3: In the wall cabinet opposite the stovetop, a built-in oven topped with a marble counter pairs with a microwave oven to create a baking center.

3

Vibrant Vision

Banishing the blahs was the impetus for reworking this kitchen into a kaleidoscope of color that is cheerful and more functional than the old drab room. Green cabinets inspired by a dishwasher advertisement kick-started the remodeling project that features new cabinets, a combination of honed granite and stainless-steel countertops, and new appliances. To save on the overall budget, the existing floors were refinished rather than replaced and much of the original floor plan was maintained. The addition of a pass-through arch between the kitchen and dining room enhances function and increases both countertop and seating space. A multicolor glass tile backsplash incorporates each of the colors used in the kitchen, unifying the bright room.

SITUATION

- Existing appliances and cabinets didn't meet current needs.
- A cramped kitchen with a sliding door to the dining room didn't have enough counterspace.
- The brown and beige decor was drab and dated.

SOLUTION

- Install new appliances and cabinets; keep the old floors to minimize unnecessary expenses.
- Replace the door with a bar, pass-through arch, and countertop and seating.
- Infuse the room with colorful cabinets, bold paint hues, and a multicolor tile backsplash.

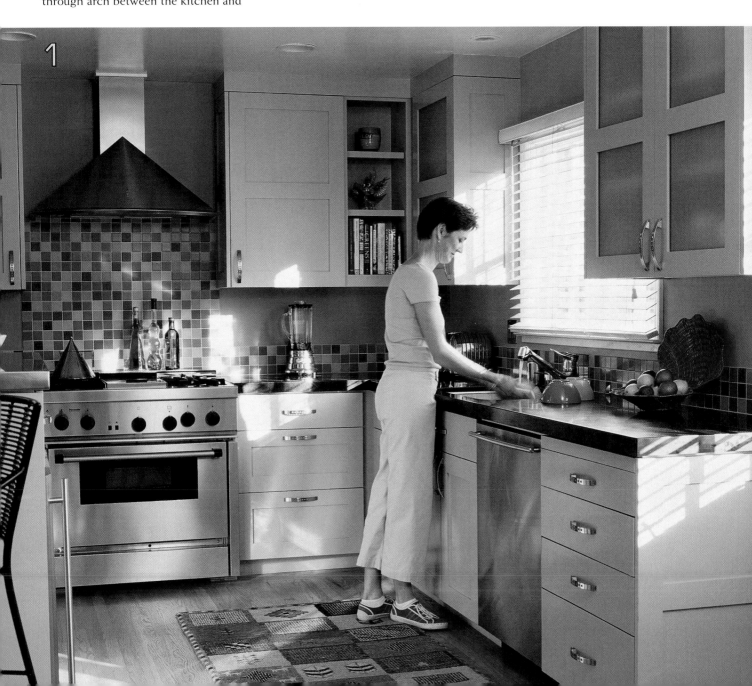

1: Green cabinets inspired by an appliance advertisement sparked this kitchen makeover. Though more costly than granite tiles, a slab of honed granite for the countertop means easier cleaning because there are no grout lines.

2: The pass-through with countertop seating is an ideal spot for snacking and studying. A sliding door was removed to provide space for a much-needed additional countertop.

3: Tall, skinny cabinet drawers take advantage of otherwise wasted space and are ideal for stowing sauce bottles.

Perfect Fit

Creating a versatile kitchen that is adaptable to almost any situation requires creativity and thoughtful planning, as exemplified by this stylish kitchen. Featuring a wall of movable glass doors, it transforms an intimate family kitchen to a large entertaining space that encompasses the dining room and breakfast nook. A lack of light was remedied by installing multiple light sources throughout the room—including a skylight, undercabinet windows, recessed task lighting, and windows that extend to the countertops. Appliance garages conceal potential clutter and conveniently group kitchen necessities such as the food processor, mixer, and microwave oven. The streamlined look allows thoughtful material choices—grained-and-burled maple cabinets, honed marble countertops, and rice paper in the glass cabinet doors—to shine.

SITUATION

- A poorly designed kitchen included four doorways, but awkward flow with the rest of the house.
- The kitchen was dark and cramped.
- Although it included the basics, nothing made this kitchen special.

SOLUTION

- Replace one wall with movable glass doors so that the kitchen, breakfast nook, and dining room can be used as one large space or closed off.
- Invite light into the room with a skylight, undercabinet windows, and windows that extend to the counter.
- Accessorize the kitchen with carefully selected materials including honed marble countertops, and grained-and-burled maple cabinets.

1: The glass doors between the kitchen and the dining room open to create one large room suitable for entertaining big groups. The dining table divides into two and attaches to each end of the breakfast table to accommodate lively dinner parties.

2: An extra-deep sink is convenient for cleaning large commercial appliance parts and oversize pots.

3: Multiple light sources paired with blond maple cabinets and honed marble countertops combine for a radiant space.

4: Subtle textures from rice paper and burled maple offer visual interest throughout.

Creative Maneuvers

Reconfiguring the room was essential for creating a better working space and improving traffic flow in this kitchen. A stairway that hampered movement in the kitchen was repositioned along an interior wall to open up enough floor space to streamline the layout of the kitchen and make space for a large island in the center of the room. To increase the room's volume, unused attic space was converted into cathedral ceilings with high windows that draw in the sunlight. Crisp white-painted cabinetry, warm cherry wood countertops, detailed trim, and wood floors provide visual warmth and add classic appeal. Informal conveniences, such as seating at the island and a breakfast room suitable for family dinners and homework, make this a natural spot for family gatherings.

SITUATION

- A small L-shape kitchen was not designed to meet the needs of a family.
- A stairway jutted into the room, creating narrow spaces that impeded traffic.
- There was no space for family dining.

SOLUTION

- Install a generous island and breakfast area for family activities and cooking.
- Reposition the staircase along an interior kitchen wall to open up floor space.
- Include informal seating at the island and add a breakfast room for family meals.

1: A large island with seating offers plenty of space for children to do homework while their parents prepare dinner. An open floor plan, a cathedral ceiling, and classic lines and materials make the kitchen inviting.

2: Tile set in a quiltlike pattern above the stove evokes country character. The range hood was built into the custom cabinets to maintain a consistent look throughout the kitchen.

2

Comfort to the Rescue

Rather than slavishly adhering to period details that didn't jibe with their more modern sensibilities, the homeowners of this 1920s English Tudor-style house took inspiration from European homes they spotted on a television show. Part of a whole-house overhaul, the kitchen is now outfitted with a comfortable mix of new, streamlined high-tech systems and original woodwork and floors. The trim received a coat of glossy white paint to pull the space out of the too-dark doldrums. The rich oak floors were sanded and refinished. Small-scale stainless-steel appliances provide efficiency without overwhelming the room. Jolts of color from green granite countertops, brightly hued accessories, and a blue and green mosaic tile backsplash enliven the space.

SITUATION

- Period design didn't live up to the desire for a high-tech kitchen.
- Dark walls and heavy window treatments weighed down the room.

SOLUTION

- Install European-inspired streamlined maple cabinets and stainless-steel appliances that fit a small room.
- Paint the trim a bright white, remove window treatments, and install a colorful glass mosaic tile backsplash to expose leaded glass.

1

1: An eclectic blend of maple cabinets, some with glass-panel inserts, green granite countertops, refinished dark oak floors, and a colorful mosaic tile backsplash offer a European-style look.

2: White trim and eggshell-color walls are punctuated with color from the table and chairs in the breakfast nook. Colorful accessories, such as the tiles painted by Salvador Dalí, are framed and hung above the entrance to the nook to add a splash of color.

3: The yellow plastic light fixture above the dining room table contrasts with the colorful, contemporary energy found in the kitchen. The '50s French sideboard along the wall is used for serving food.

Esteem Makeover

A tight, compartmentalized kitchen, pantry, and breakfast room didn't fit with the rest of this grand 2,500-square-foot house. With plenty of total living space in the house, the kitchen needed to live larger rather than grow larger. Tearing down the wall between the kitchen and breakfast room and eliminating the closed-off pantry provided the space for more smart changes. A multiuse peninsula provides an additional work surface and storage accessible from two sides. Two tall, narrow cabinets that extend to the ceiling keep the rest of the room free from upper cabinets and emphasize the high ceilings that make the space appear larger. The refrigerator that once couldn't open without making one half of the kitchen inaccessible now resides just outside the work core, yet still close enough for easy access. Base cabinets stained cherry ground the room with warm wood tones. Soft gray walls and white cabinets, tile, and woodwork create a lofty feeling of spaciousness.

SITUATION

- A cramped 8×13-foot kitchen didn't function in an otherwise grand home.
- Upper cabinets made the narrow kitchen seem even more enclosed.
- Opening the refrigerator blocked passage from one end of the kitchen to the other.

SOLUTION

- Remove a wall between the kitchen and breakfast room to create a larger single space without adding square footage.
- Define the work core without closing it off by adding a multiuse peninsula.
- Move the refrigerator to the location of a former walk-in pantry to open space in the work core while keeping the appliance close.

1: Preserving existing window locations in the kitchen and breakfast area allows natural light to enter both spaces from two directions. Positioning the refrigerator just outside the work core opens up counterspace while still keeping the appliance conveniently located.

2: White upper cabinets visually recede, especially when partnered with cherry base cabinets. The tall units on the sink wall and peninsula allow the rest of the upper walls to remain free of cabinetry.

Global Expansion

Combining three separate rooms into one spacious kitchen provides the opportunity for state-of-the-art features and global design flair. The former kitchen was chopped up into three too-small rooms— pantry, kitchen, and breakfast room. The previous configuration didn't offer enough space for essential appliances so the pantry inconveniently housed the refrigerator. Now the 11×21-foot remodeled kitchen boasts a professional-style cooktop, oven, and hood; a double-bowl, stainless-steel sink; and two dishwasher drawers, all on one wall. The opposite wall houses three banks of wide drawers, a large pantry cabinet, and a sleek stainless-steel refrigerator. There's twice as much countertop and storage space as before. And the new room features international design inspiration that plays homage to the homeowners' global lifestyles and heritages. Natural maple cabinets paired with black granite countertops provide an Asian look, while the terra-cotta walls are inspired by Italian architecture.

SITUATION

- A too-small kitchen didn't fit a busy family.
- The space was divided into a separate pantry, kitchen, and breakfast area.
- Expanses of upper cabinets made a narrow room seem confining.

SOLUTION

- Annex space from adjoining areas to create a kitchen big enough for cooks, kids, and friends.
- Combine the spaces to allow room for an eat-in kitchen big enough for efficient storage and work space.
- Minimize the number of upper cabinets to accentuate the openness.

1: The peninsula opposite the French doors offers seating and dining space in the kitchen.

2: Reconfiguring three separate spaces into one large kitchen provided room for French doors to a patio.

3: Maple cabinets are sectioned by cedar posts for Asian-inspired style.

From Awkward to Artsy

Working smarter rather than building larger was the motto for this renovation. To create an open, airy floor plan, efficient, space-saving refrigerator drawers replaced a bulky commercial appliance. Sleek yet strong steel shelves attached to wall studs eliminate the need for boxy, space-grabbing wall cabinets. An awkward peninsula that previously divided the 10×14-foot kitchen from the 10×10-foot dining room was removed, creating an open family-friendly space. A cozy corner banquette now opens to the kitchen and offers a place for meals, homework, and family time. Maple base cabinets finished with a dark mahogany and black stain, concrete countertops and backsplash, and stainless-steel shelving offer a contemporary Euro-style look. A cheerful ocher-hue paint accents the wall behind the sink, imbuing the kitchen with warmth.

SITUATION

- Boxy wall cabinets made the kitchen feel too enclosed.
- The small cooking area was divided from the dining area.
- A 1960s remodeling made the room look dated.

SOLUTION

- Replace space-stealing wall-mounted cabinets with open stainless-steel shelves.
- Remove an awkward peninsula to open up the cooking and eating areas.
- Add sleek cabinets, concrete countertops, and an ocher-color accent wall for contemporary style.

1: Refrigerator drawers take up less space than a full-size appliance and provide easy access.

2: Built-in seating can accommodate 10 people and offers the family ample space for homework. Pillows of washable suede and easy-care cotton ensure quick cleanup. Extra storage is tucked underneath for school supplies and paperwork.

3: To allow more light into the kitchen upper cabinets were replaced with sleek stainless-steel shelves. Attached to the studs, the shelves span the existing windows.

4: The varying thickness of the concrete countertop and color gradations on the walls make for a visually appealing kitchen.

Vintage Vitality

Vintage style doesn't eschew a family-friendly floor plan and modern conveniences as this kitchen in a historic neighborhood aptly demonstrates. A poorly executed 1950s renovation left the kitchen out of step with the home's 1930s-era character. While the earlier remodeling project undid the charm of the original cabinets, appliances, and surfaces, the original footprint was left intact.

A fresh approach to remaking the kitchen involved removing the wall between the kitchen and breakfast room to create one open area that fills both spaces with more light. A peninsula where the wall once stood provides additional work and storage space. Eliminating a walk-in pantry and one of two swinging doors to the dining room offers additional space for cabinetry and countertops and allows for more efficient appliance placement.

The goal for the rest of the project was to restore vintage charm and historically accurate details. A half-century-old range left by the previous homeowners was restored to like-new appearance and good working order and is now the focal point of the room. Nickel-finish latches, bin-style pulls, and glass knobs adorn recessed-panel cabinets. Light fixtures feature period parts including amethyst glass. New fixtures, such as the faucet, have period-faithful elements including a wall-mount design, dual handles, and a gooseneck spout. Even modern features such as refrigerator drawers feature a cloak of period style with Shaker-style fronts. The kitchen is designed to meet today's needs with style that should withstand the test of time.

SITUATION

- A 1950s renovation removed the character from the 1936 kitchen.
- Floor plan problems common to a 1936 kitchen were not addressed in an earlier renovation.

SOLUTION

- Restore its original style using a photo of a period kitchen as a model.
- Improve the floor plan by removing the wall between the kitchen and breakfast area.

2

3

1: This new faucet yields period-appropriate style, making it perfect for pairing with a large apron-front sink.

2: True antiques, reproductions, and modern conveniences combine in this vintage-style kitchen. Dishwasher drawers, for example, are disguised by panels that match the Shaker-style cabinets.

3: Refrigerator drawers keep produce and snacks close to the cooking and breakfast areas.

1: Removing the wall between the breakfast area and kitchen brings more light into both areas and prevents the kitchen from feeling dark and cramped.

2: A local firm restored the old range that came with the house.

3: A paneled front and strategic placement in the corner blends the refrigerator seamlessly into the vintage look of the kitchen.

1

2

3

Pushing the Limits

Canny color, savvy storage, and floor plan finesse took this room to the hilt. Although the homeowners were desperate for storage, they didn't want to enlarge their modest kitchen. Removing an interior wall united the area with adjoining dining and living rooms, but it meant sacrificing cabinet and appliance space. To compensate, a new island houses a cooktop, wine rack, drawers, and microwave oven. Solid-door cabinets near the ceiling boost storage. The microwave oven tucks under the cooktop, which forms a work triangle with the sink and built-in refrigerator. The woodsy cabinetry hues and stainless-steel appliances help the kitchen blend with nearby living spaces.

SITUATION

- A kitchen with no chance of expansion needed room for improvement.
- An existing lack of storage space could be exacerbated after the planned removal of an interior wall.
- With plans to open the kitchen to other living spaces, the original style would be out of step with adjoining rooms.

SOLUTION

- Remove an interior wall to open the kitchen to the dining and living room.
- Add an island to house appliances and drawers. Add cabinets at ceiling line.
- Install honey- and mint-hued cabinetry and cover the refrigerator with cabinet-matching panels for a unified look.

1: A window with a sill too low for cabinets and counters makes a perfect spot for a built-in desk. Frosted-glass cabinet doors add to the kitchen's open-face character.

2: New honey- and mint-color cabinets invigorate a 20-year-old kitchen. The island cooktop's downdraft exhaust cut out the need for a view-blocking hood.

3: A glass-door cabinet shows off a collection of vintage pottery. Oak flooring radiates the same woodsy warmth as the wall cabinetry.

Cutting Corners with Style

Removing a closet allowed this once-cramped room to expand into a comfortable eat-in kitchen. The happy discovery of a pocket of dead space—and eliminating it—allowed for much-needed extra storage. Once the space was expanded, the appliance layout was reconfigured in an L shape more conducive to food prep and cooking than the previous galley's row of appliances along one wall. A careful review of building codes and city ordinances revealed that the range could be positioned in front of an existing window, saving the cost of repositioning or eliminating the opening. Additional money-saving tactics include substituting marble tiles for a slab on the counters, edging the counters with inexpensive aluminum, and using engineered wood flooring rather than individual oak planks. The resulting savings left money in the budget to splurge on semicustom cabinetry with stainless-steel hardware. The rich, dark cabinets with Craftsman-like detailing blend with the architecture of the 1929 house.

SITUATION

- The appliances were arranged in one long galleylike strip making prep work and cooking uncomfortable.
- The space was too small for a table and chairs, forcing a young family to eat in a formal dining room.
- A prior remodel left the kitchen looking dated.

SOLUTION

- Remove a closet and knock down functionless walls to create a larger eat-in kitchen.
- Arrange appliances in an L shape to maximize efficiency for prep work and cooking and make space for a table.

- Semicustom cabinetry with stainless-steel hardware fast-forwards the kitchen into the present.

1: Removing an old closet and dead space left room for a comfortable dining nook. Taking the cabinets to the ceiling creates a custom look.

2: Rich wood cabinets maintain the architectural style found elsewhere in the 1929 house. Modern stainless-steel appliances offer 21st-century convenience and an overall eclectic look.

3: Building codes allowed the range to be positioned under the existing kitchen window, which saved money. Using the same marble tiles as those used in the bathroom lends impact and continuity to the kitchen counters.

3

Universal Design

Universal design makes a house more livable and functional for people of all ages and abilities. Many homeowners incorporate universal design concepts into their homes whether they need them now or are planning for the future. Make your kitchen user-friendly by identifying irritating barriers for anyone in a wheelchair or with a physical limitation. Are cabinets and other appliances out of reach? Do oven doors drop open and block access to racks? Are countertops too high or appliance knobs and faucets difficult to operate? Follow our list of universal design principles to ensure everyone can enjoy your kitchen for years to come.

Aisles and Approach Room. You'll need 48-inch aisles—which is often recommended for multicook kitchens—and 60 inches of space for wheelchair turnaround.

Appliances. For safety, select wall ovens. Be sure to factor in room for landing space for hot pans and casseroles directly beside or in front of the oven. Select a separate cooktop with pull-up space beneath and front-mounted controls for easy access. Smooth glass-top cooktops allow a cook to slide pots and pans easily. Choose a side-by-side refrigerator model that gives a seated cook easy access.

Comfortable Reach. Door handles, appliances, electrical switches, and outlets should be located 15 to 48 inches above the floor so anyone can reach them comfortably.

Cabinetry and Storage. Choose finishes that hide dings and marks. Install cabinet doors to slide horizontally rather than pointing outward. Plot plenty of storage in lower cabinets—pullout shelves are key for bringing contents into view and within reach. Select wide pulls rather than knobs to help those with hand-strength or dexterity problems.

Counterspace. Plot ample stretches of countertop wherever possible, especially next to the refrigerator, oven, stove, and sink. Installing a continuous line of countertop absent of any obstructions from the refrigerator to the sink to the cooktop allows the cook to slide mixing and cooking vessels from one workspace to another. Don't forget to leave ample knee space underneath the counter to accommodate wheelchair users.

Countertops. Bullnose fronts and rounded corners reduce injury and help those who use a wheelchair "shove off" from the counter with just an elbow or forearm. Keep most countertops at the standard height; to accommodate a person in a wheelchair, consider lowering a section of countertop such as an island or peninsula.

Faucets and Handles. Mount faucets to the side rather than at the back to eliminate long reaches. A gooseneck faucet or one with a retractable or pullout spray head makes filling tall pots easier. Lever-handle faucets provide control of water temperature and flow—the longer the handle, the better. Consider hands-free faucets that turn on with a sensor for even more ease.

Floors and Thresholds. Choose a material that's firm and smooth—but not slippery. Eliminate bumpy thresholds.

Knee Clearances and Toe-Kicks. Wheelchair users require knee clearances of 27 inches high, 30 inches wide, and 19 inches deep. Extra-large 9×6-inch toe-kicks allow chair users to pull up closer.

Sinks. Select a shallow basin that drains at the back to allow adequate knee space. The area beneath the basin should be insulated to protect legs and feet from contact with hot and cold water pipes.

2

1: A sink and peninsula placed 30 inches high rather than the standard 36 allow wheelchair accessibility. Including accessibility doesn't mean sacrificing style, as evidenced by these custom-designed pocket doors beneath the sink. When open, they allow wheelchair access; when closed, they look just like the rest of the kitchen's cabinetry.

2: Open space below a lowered cooktop accommodates a wheelchair, while custom cherry and maple cabinetry creates a sophisticated look. Cooking utensils hang from hooks to the right of the cooktop for easy access, and counter space on each side means some prep work can be completed at the stove.

Simply Perfect Storage

With so much stuff to stash away in a kitchen, it's no wonder storage is such an important function. Perishable and nonperishable food items, tableware, pots and pans, cooking utensils, small appliances, cookbooks, and more all require space. The right amount, the right kind, and perhaps most significantly, the right placement of storage are central to an efficient kitchen that's a pleasure to work in.

Commit to a clutter-free kitchen by taking advantage of the new products and solutions that provide more storage options than ever before. Many of these innovations, which were originally developed for high-end commercial and custom kitchens, are now available as off-the-shelf options for kitchens everywhere. A truly masterful storage arrangement means you'll be able to take advantage of every spare inch of prime kitchen space.

1: Open, contemporary stainless-steel shelving has moved from industrial-size gourmet kitchens into cozy homes, in this case ensuring that the family chef doesn't have to reach into cabinets for plates when dinner is hot.

2: Roll-out pantry cabinets store a plethora of canned and boxed staples in a compact area.

3: Knife drawers with custom cutouts accommodate specific knives, ensuring that they are safely stashed and will stay sharper longer.

4: Stainless-steel tambour doors roll up to provide access to the microwave oven, toaster oven, and apothecary drawers in this baking area.

5: Handy slide-out baskets are a stylish break from cabinets and keep fruits and vegetables nearby. Open shelves also offer an ideal place to organize with handsome wicker, plastic, or metal baskets.

6: A small drawer for linens with space below for trays and baking pans exemplifies the wealth of efficient storage that can be built into a compact kitchen.

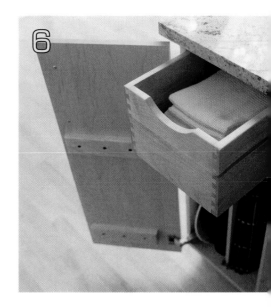

1: Everything has a place in this Colonial kitchen with cupboards, apothecary drawers, and items hanging from a ceiling rack.

2: Wrinkled towels, runners, and tablecloths are a thing of the past when linens are kept neatly draped over dowels. Any base cabinet can handle the duty when equipped with a rack that pulls out.

3: For a change of pace, shelves zigzag down a narrow wine cabinet near an appliance garage.

Whether you're gutting and reworking your current kitchen or starting from scratch in a new home, remember that it's all about obtaining livability, style, and hardworking function. Choose materials and fixtures wisely so your new kitchen looks beautiful and performs well. This gallery of possibilities is a great start to figuring out what your brand-new kitchen needs—and what you want.

make new

Open Minded

Crafting a kitchen with fewer than four walls—while ensuring it possesses definition, storage options, and style—may be the ultimate design challenge. Or it might be a breeze, when savvy planning produces a U-shape cooking area bordered by peninsulas. The peninsulas, along with ceiling-mounted cabinets, provide storage and work surfaces without blocking views of the surrounding rooms and the ocean beyond the home's windows. The warm look of maple and cherry cabinetry balances the cool character of a stainless-steel backsplash and appliances. Only the room's performance rivals its style—plenty of storage and a compact work area behind a modest-size island ensure

the blue pearl granite countertops remain clutter-free.

SITUATION

- The homeowners wanted to open their kitchen to the adjacent living and dining areas.
- The newly planned visible kitchen would have to blend with surrounding spaces.

SOLUTION

- Create a wall-less, U-shape cooking area bordered by peninsulas and ceiling-mounted cabinets.
- Build cabinetry from the same wood used elsewhere in the home; select glass cabinet inserts that repeat the shape of exterior windows.

1: Granite countertops define the kitchen's domain, while the cantilevered section with barstools blurs the line between bar and breakfast table. Fluted-glass inserts add visual interest to the ceiling-mounted cabinets.

2: Two peninsulas and a modest-size island buffer the step-saving U-shape cooking area from people seated nearby.

Cottage Turnaround

The rambling cottage's entire first floor—including the kitchen—lacked personality and presence. The only remedy, the homeowners decided, was to flip around the arrangement of the rooms. In the process of rearranging, out went the kitchen's pink laminate countertops and heavy upper cabinetry. In came a tall bank of windows, rift-sawn golden-oak floors, and a hefty island that serves as a command post for a busy family. The new location captures views and sunlight, making the kitchen a natural magnet for the whole family.

SITUATION

- Closed off to the rest of the first floor, the kitchen didn't draw anyone in.
- The kitchen's location didn't take advantage of spectacular views outside.
- Pink countertops and dark upper cabinetry made for a dreary space.

SOLUTION

- Rearrange rooms, opening the kitchen to nearby breakfast and living areas.
- Create a bank of windows along one wall to welcome in light and views.
- Pair bright white cabinetry with subdued countertops.

1: Twin dishwashers near the sink handle the many dishes of a busy family of six.

2: Authentic Craftsman touches in the dining room cabinets include wavy glass in cabinet doors and canted support pillars.

3: In lieu of upper cabinetry, the homeowners chose a wall of windows that let light into the kitchen. The stamped stainless-steel backsplash above the stove shines in the natural light.

Oceanfront Wonder

Living large in a home that's only 25 feet wide takes some creative planning. In this case it meant demolishing a cramped second-floor galley kitchen and master suite to make way for a more spacious, open layout that allows a kitchen, dining area, and family room to mix freely. A gleaming, professional-caliber range anchors the new kitchen like an old-fashioned hearth. Throughout the space, blue and green accents and sleek surfaces suggest qualities of water, while the marble floor is the color of sand. A granite island with a raised breakfast bar acts as a boundary, not a barrier, ensuring the cook's quarters and family area remain one.

SITUATION

- A narrow home left few options for expanding a tiny, dark kitchen.
- The home sits on a tight lot, which meant neighbors were too close for comfort.
- The California kitchen needed ties to its oceanfront location.

SOLUTION

- Combine the kitchen, dining area, and library into an open living area.
- Replace existing side windows with larger units made of translucent laminated white glass for privacy.
- Select flooring the color of sand and blue and green accents reminiscent of water.

1: Windows fitted with white laminate glass admit breezes and light into the kitchen while blocking views of nearby neighbors.

2: Pale cabinets with etched-glass inserts and dark green granite countertops combine to echo the moods of sand and sea.

3: The removal of several walls combines the kitchen, dining area, and family room.

Eat-In Escape

Once the doors fell off the kitchen cabinets, it was time to remodel. Preservation of the original layout and detailing of the Shingle-style house became a priority as the house was stripped to its studs and rebuilt. In the eat-in kitchen, this involved creating connections with the surrounding rooms, including the sunny breakfast nook and family room. Tomato-red walls, natural cherry cabinets, and quartersawn oak floors make the kitchen a warm cocoon, while elements such as the stainless-steel appliances and art-tile backsplash fit the midcentury modern style of the rest of the home.

SITUATION

- A tight layout made the compact kitchen seem closed off from the rest of the home.
- At 12×12 feet, the cook's work area wasn't big enough.

SOLUTION

- Create easy connections with surrounding rooms, including a winding staircase leading to the second floor and a 30×40-inch pass-through to the adjacent family room.
- Create room for a snack bar, which lets guests chat with the cook without invading the work zone.

1: The backsplash behind the stainless-steel range features a twigs-and-berry pattern that complements the tomato-red walls and cherry cabinets.

2: Cherry molding and oak floors marry the breakfast nook to the kitchen. The cheery yellow chairs echo the midcentury style found throughout the home.

3: A snack bar lets guests chat with the cook without getting in the way of food preparations. A curving back stairway links the kitchen to the bedrooms above.

Vacation Inspiration

A top-to-bottom renovation turned a sweet but tired rental cottage into a lakefront family spot. Removing the claustrophobic warren of rooms on the main level opened the space to views stretching past the kitchen and living room to the backyard deck. See-through upper cabinets in front of the windows keep the space bright even on dreary days. White-oak floor planks and painted cabinets with curved feet create cottage charm. By selecting midrange stainless-steel appliances, the homeowners were able to afford luxurious granite countertops. To complete the space, a centrally located island with a cooktop provides extra counter space for cooking or dining.

SITUATION

- Part of a choppy collection of rooms, the kitchen was wedged into a back corner of the home.
- A cottage kitchen craves natural light—and this one had almost none.
- The vacation home needed cottage style but within a reasonable budget.

SOLUTION

- Make the kitchen an open, central area nestled between the dining and living rooms.
- Install see-through cabinets in front of the windows to usher in light and capitalize on storage space.
- When possible, use stock windows, reasonably-priced cabinets, and midrange appliance models.

1: See-through storage fills the cottage-style kitchen with light and ensures even a busy cook can enjoy lakefront views.

2: Stock windows and custom cabinets combine to create a striking display space. A pullout in the toe-kick to the left of the sink harbors a flip-up step stool so small children can reach the farmhouse-style sink.

3: The new, open floor plan creates a seamless transition between the dining, kitchen, and living areas.

Points of View

1: The breakfast table is situated to take advantage of spectacular views. A new set of French doors connects the kitchen to the side yard.

2: Drawers in the island keep previously hard-to-store items such as tablecloths and place mats neat and accessible. Short cabinets above the refrigerator hold items used infrequently.

3: Placing a powerful range hood above the range meant sacrificing storage, but plenty of lower and upper cabinets on the other walls help.

The 1930s Tudor house was surrounded by stunning vistas, but the spectacular scene wasn't visible from the uninteresting kitchen until a new two-story addition made room for a plethora of windows to welcome in light. Now a bank of windows behind the range funnels light throughout the family-size kitchen and breakfast nook. The wall of windows sacrifices storage, so plenty of storage is located elsewhere—in drawers and shelves in the island, in the pantry, and in upper and lower cabinetry along the walls. Staying true to the home's original style, architectural flourishes such as arched passages between rooms and the gritty surface of the plaster walls ensure new and old gels.

SITUATION

- The home set on an idyllic site didn't measure up to its panoramic surroundings.
- The new kitchen needed to stay true to the rest of the 1935 Tudor home.

SOLUTION

- Build a new two-story addition that includes a kitchen and breakfast area with walls of windows.
- Match new materials to old—the oak flooring and mahogany moldings in the kitchen blend with the original flooring and molding found elsewhere.

1: Combined with the dining and living rooms, the kitchen
forms a large living space for weekend entertaining.

2: The kitchen opens to the dining room and views of the bay
beyond the screen porch.

Summertime Charm

The requirements for this cottage kitchen were clear even before construction began on the new summer house. At the top of the list: an open floor plan that caters to a couple or a crowd, allowing for communal cooking as well as space for noncooks to gather nearby.

The plan integrates the kitchen with the dining and living rooms to create one generous space. This concept makes sense for a summer cottage because cooking and eating with family and friends is such a pivotal part of the weekend experience. The combined space suits big crowds, although the 10×16-foot kitchen itself is comparatively small. To perform at peak efficiency, the island serves as the main prep area. A bookcase at one end of the island and a wine rack at the other provide a generous surface for multiple cooks, while one side of the island includes seating for spectators. For added storage, a vintage-style hutch combines the functionality of a pantry with the display space of a china cabinet.

A key component of the kitchen is, of course, its cottage styling. Crown molding tops the white, lightly distressed cabinets. In contrast to the peppy, playful blue and white checkerboard backsplash, the range hood's carved inlays add a bit of Victorian finery. Overhead, decorative boxed ceiling beams strike a balance between rustic and refined. A mahogany-stained oak floor—which ties the kitchen with the dining and living areas—will age as gracefully as the rest of the summer home.

2

SITUATION

- The brand-new summer home required the intimacy of a country cottage as well as space for weekend entertaining.
- Although the kitchen exuded country style, contemporary details were desired.
- Cooks and noncooks alike needed to feel welcome.

SOLUTION

- Open the compact alley kitchen to the surrounding living areas.
- Choose stainless-steel appliances and a galvanized sheet metal tabletop.
- Include seating along one side of the island and situate the refrigerator so guests can nab beverages or snacks.

1: Big and small stainless-steel appliances provide contemporary contrast to the classic white tile and cabinetry of the cottage-style kitchen.

2: The island sink located close to the dishwasher is ideal for cleanup as well as prep work.

3: The island provides storage—including a wine rack tucked in one end—as well as plenty of space for guests to sit while cooks work.

Small Yet Mighty

Everything had cracks and pulled seams until a masterful makeover turned an outdated kitchen into a stylish workspace decked out in an eclectic mix of vintage and clean-lined elements. The homeowners measured everything from aluminum foil packages to cookie sheets to pinpoint their storage needs before peeling the kitchen back to its studs and making three critical moves. First they relocated the water heater to the attic to make space for a commercial range. Next they borrowed 6 inches from the bathroom closet behind the refrigerator so the hefty appliance sits flush with the dishwasher. Finally, they closed off an exterior doorway to create an uninterrupted wall for storage and a countertop. The finished kitchen possesses vintage style and enough elbowroom for two cooks.

SITUATION

- A tiny kitchen required creative storage ideas so everything would have a place.
- Although they were planning to gut the entire kitchen, the homeowners wanted to maintain its country style.

SOLUTION

- Stash everything from kitchen linens to produce in old wire gym baskets on open shelves; install large, deep drawers and cupboards to organize other items.
- Use a wax finish and chrome pulls and latches to create cabinetry with a rich, antiqued look.

1: This renovated country kitchen houses many storage options, from open shelving and cabinetry above to pullout drawers and wire baskets below.

2: Antique punched tin ceiling tiles in their original color comprise the backsplash behind the sink.

3: Chrome pulls and latches add country style to the antique-finish cabinets. The light fixture is one of two former warehouse fixtures found at a salvage shop.

Sunny Disposition

After an ill-conceived 1970s renovation left this galley kitchen clad in floor-to-ceiling linoleum, a yellow refrigerator, and brown appliances, a pair of do-it-yourselfers chose to return the space to its original Arts and Crafts style. Gutting an old kitchen layout and borrowing space from an adjacent bedroom garnered elbowroom. Smooth

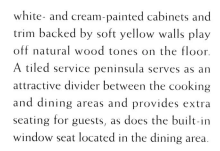

white- and cream-painted cabinets and trim backed by soft yellow walls play off natural wood tones on the floor. A tiled service peninsula serves as an attractive divider between the cooking and dining areas and provides extra seating for guests, as does the built-in window seat located in the dining area.

SITUATION

- The choppy layout of the 1910 home carried into the kitchen, which was plagued by limited storage and space.
- A 1970s remodel erased the original Arts and Crafts style of the space.
- With little room in the work space, guests needed a place to sit.

SOLUTION

- Borrow space from an adjacent room and open the kitchen to the dining area.
- Add Arts and Crafts details, such as Mission-style pendent lights and Shaker-style cabinetry.
- Add a tiled peninsula with an overhang for stools in the kitchen and build a cushioned window seat in the adjacent dining area.

1: The wall-size hutch, designed to resemble a piece of freestanding furniture, boasts the same cabinet door style found in the dining room. Its tiled alcove harbors favorite display pieces.

2: A window seat allows for easy interaction with the chef, while the surrounding storage areas stow everything from linens to dog food.

3: A white and yellow color scheme carries through the Arts and Crafts style kitchen in everything from the backsplash tile and range hood to the pottery displayed on the open shelving.

4: The 4×6-foot pantry provides storage for less-frequently used appliances.

Polished Patina

When a steady stream of family members and guests traipse through the kitchen work area, it's hard for the resident cook to accomplish anything. Closing this kitchen's old entry and flip-flopping the work core helped reroute traffic. Now the kitchen is a series of family-friendly zones with a sunny central hallway.

To return the kitchen to its original vintage charm, the homeowners fixed the sagging floor, evened out the multilevel ceiling, got rid of an awkward column in the middle of the kitchen, and opened the load-bearing walls for banks of new windows. Moldings and columns were added, while some of the old doors were kept to maintain

period-correct style. Because windows were chosen in place of upper cabinets, appliance drawers are tucked under the fossilized-limestone countertops.

The walls are painted taupe, and the cabinets are a subtly mottled gray to keep the color scheme neutral. The custom-finish cabinetry is flecked with flakes of real silver and copper to

1: A stainless-steel hood and quilted backsplash give the 48-inch-wide range back-to-hearth appeal. The kitchen nimbly mixes old and new.

2: The cleanup zone—which includes an end cabinet stowing dishes and utensils near the table—also serves as a breakfast area complete with espresso maker and toaster.

create texture, depth, and subtle color variation. The cabinets blend with the limestone countertops and stainless-steel elements, such as the dual-fuel ovens and refrigerator drawers, to create a high-tech space with a historical past.

SITUATION

- Family and guests entering the kitchen landed right in the middle of the work core.
- A 1980s kitchen redo erased the vintage charm present elsewhere in the home.
- Planned additional windows instead of upper cabinets would leave little room for storage near the work space.

SOLUTION

- Flip the floor plan and widen the foyer to open up a new route to the kitchen.
- Add classic crown moldings and columns and preserve some of the old doors.
- Tuck appliance and cabinet drawers under the countertops to carry the storage load.

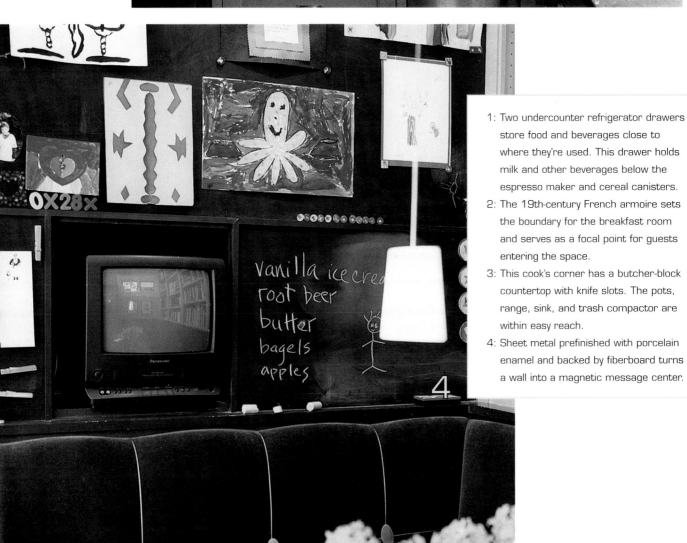

1: Two undercounter refrigerator drawers store food and beverages close to where they're used. This drawer holds milk and other beverages below the espresso maker and cereal canisters.

2: The 19th-century French armoire sets the boundary for the breakfast room and serves as a focal point for guests entering the space.

3: This cook's corner has a butcher-block countertop with knife slots. The pots, range, sink, and trash compactor are within easy reach.

4: Sheet metal prefinished with porcelain enamel and backed by fiberboard turns a wall into a magnetic message center.

Bright Ideas

Instead of acting as the accommodating hub of family life, this formerly clumsy kitchen often caused traffic to stop right in the middle of a busy cook's work area. The solution lay in gutting the existing kitchen and several adjacent areas to unscramble traffic patterns, and in replacing the restrictive peninsula in favor of a new compact island. Another bonus: Cutting corners, adding windows, and projecting the sink area into the yard created a sunlit corner that evokes the atmosphere of an enclosed porch. The new kitchen and adjacent nook are inspired by Victorian homes of the past, yet they convey decidedly modern touches. Traditional millwork and cabinetry exude a casual sense of style thanks to a muted green color palette with bright red and marigold accents. Family-practical touches such as snacks stored at kid-friendly height in the eating nook and an organization center tucked at the side entry ensure the kitchen is loaded with everything kids, pets, and parents need.

SITUATION

- A convoluted layout meant people were always traipsing through the kitchen.
- A modern family needed more storage than vintage cabinetry could deliver.
- The awkward peninsula hindered travel through and work within the kitchen.

SOLUTION

- Create a new layout that redirects traffic so it runs alongside—not through—the kitchen.
- Install vintage-look cabinetry that accommodates modern needs—such as recycling bins reminiscent of old-fashioned flour bins.
- Remove the peninsula in favor of a compact island loaded with storage.

1: The top coat of the red table is purposely worn away in areas to reveal a dark green undercoat, further contributing to the space's casual atmosphere.

2: Pullout shelves near the dishwasher store dishes at a convenient height. The compact island stores more than some twice its size.

3: Corner windows that surround the sink area fill the new kitchen with light.

3

Gourmet Gallery

One of the most significant kitchen trends in recent years has been the migration of commercial-grade products and materials into residential kitchens. Professional chefs have long enjoyed the benefits of high-powered burners, dual-fuel ranges, and easy-to-clean stainless appliances. Today, commercial-grade appliances and materials are increasingly available at retail outlets, making it easy for anyone to incorporate gourmet features into a kitchen.

The trend goes way beyond function: Commercial kitchens have become a full-blown aesthetic that

1: Even this traditionally styled kitchen packs a gourmet punch with a built-in espresso maker paired with a stainless-steel toaster to create a convenient breakfast station.

2: Refrigerator drawers in a highly used work zone maximize the efficiency of any kitchen.

3: Stacked stainless-steel dishwasher drawers tucked between kitchen cabinets near the sink add a sophisticated element to an earth-toned kitchen and make cleanup easy.

4: The counter peninsula in this vintage bistro kitchen boasts a butcher-block top, knife storage area, and narrow wine refrigerator. The stainless-steel shelves on the wall match the room's appliances and cabinet hardware.

celebrates high-quality industrial materials, sleek surfaces, and rugged good looks. Manufacturers of consumer-grade products are following suit, cladding home appliances in commercial-look surfaces. Meanwhile inventive homeowners are finding ways to repurpose commercial products, such as shelving and storage units, and industrial materials, including glass slabs, concrete, and galvanized steel, in creative ways to enhance both the function and the form of their kitchens. Use the following examples to inspire and incorporate gourmet style into your own cookspace.

1: Stainless-steel appliances—including a stainless-steel range, spice rack, refrigerator, microwave oven, and double oven on an adjacent wall—power the contemporary look of this kitchen.

2: The warming drawer below the microwave oven in this island holds baked goods or side dishes at the appropriate temperature until the rest of the meal is ready.

3: A convenient swing-arm pot-filler faucet above the range eliminates the hassle of carrying heavy pots of water from the main sink.

4: This stainless-steel prep sink and faucet reflect the contemporary glow of the granite countertop. Island prep sinks are common fixtures in gourmet kitchens.

Eating Options

1

No kitchen is complete without an accompanying dining area in which to enjoy the fruits (and vegetables) of your labor. What type of eating space you choose depends on how you wish to use it. Even if you have a separate dining area for more formal meals, plan for a casual eating space in the kitchen. If your family's busy schedule requires quick meals, consider an island or peninsula that seats everyone. Do you regularly sit down to family dinners together? Place a table in or near the kitchen, or add a space-saving built-in banquette.

When planning eat-in spaces, ensure your table or island and seating options coordinate with the kitchen. For a contemporary space, consider a glass-topped table with stainless-steel chairs; a country kitchen might require mismatched chairs gathered around a painted wooden table. Make certain stools at islands or peninsulas are in proportion so guests aren't sitting too high or too low. Elements such as pillows or seat cushions should coordinate with your kitchen color scheme.

1: This roomy island serves as the main food preparation area and—thanks to a 15-inch overhang on each of its four sides—seats as many as eight for casual meals.

2: A built-in banquette and trestle table accommodates up to nine for dining and afternoon homework activities. Pillows that match the room's color scheme soften the built-in bench.

3: This kitchen easily transitions from a cooking to dining area with a rustic rectangular table and contemporary white chairs. The table blends with the aged brick and wood elements, while the chairs are a nod to white walls and stainless-steel cabinetry.

1: A half-round eating nook throws a contemporary curve into a kitchen with a mostly traditional lineup of right angles and straight edges. Windows fill the semicircular banquette with warm light.

2: Paired with woven-seat wood stools, an extra-wide limestone counter doubles as a breakfast bar. Nearby, a small corner nook offers a relaxed eating area.

3: Nestled between the family room and dining area, this compact kitchen boasts a two-level countertop that places diners on one side and cooks on the other. The distinct counter areas, which seat four diners altogether, are separated by fluted columns and classical arches.

The recipe for a great kitchen of any size or style includes a mix of just the right ingredients. In this chapter you'll find a review of appliances, cabinetry, countertops, sinks and faucets, flooring, and light fixtures—the staple elements from which every kitchen is composed. The word of the day is variety: There are more products, types, and styles with more features and functions than ever before.

kitchen elements

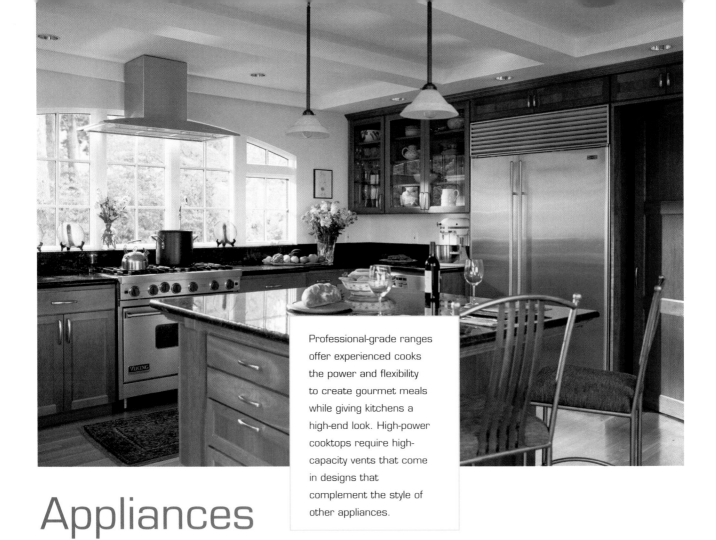

Professional-grade ranges offer experienced cooks the power and flexibility to create gourmet meals while giving kitchens a high-end look. High-power cooktops require high-capacity vents that come in designs that complement the style of other appliances.

Appliances

Appliance selection can be exciting and overwhelming. The right appliances significantly enhance the cooking experience. A growing range of options and features for most appliances virtually ensures you can find what you need and want. Because appliances are one of the biggest costs in a kitchen project and should last for years, it's important to make an informed choice.

GETTING STARTED

The best starting point for selecting appliances is to determine your cooking needs. Are you an avid cook with the budget to support top-of-the-line features? Perhaps you have a busy family and are cost conscious—if so, reasonably priced appliances will likely please you. If you dream of a gourmet-look, showcase kitchen, professional and commercial-look appliances are widely available. Most of these pieces demand plenty of space and—with ranges and cooktops—proper venting

and sometimes a stronger substructure to support their weight.

Also consider design preferences when selecting appliances. You likely fall into one of two groups: those who want appliances to disappear completely or those who want them to stand out. Manufacturers oblige on both counts. Some appliances integrate into the cabinetry with low-profile lines that don't show the controls. Their inconspicuous panel fronts match cabinetry; radius-edge styling and curved corners help ease the transition between cabinetry and appliances. On the other hand, big, beefy, stainless-steel appliances that mimic commercial styling address the desire to make appliances a focal point.

Regardless of your choice, a host of functional innovations means faster cooking, easier cleanup, and greater durability. Here are some of the options and latest developments you'll encounter when shopping.

COOKTOPS AND BURNERS

Traditional electric and gas burners are available, along with a host of improvements and high-tech options.

Traditional gas burners offer unsurpassed control, instant on and off, economy of operation, and visual evidence of heat levels.

Sealed gas burners contain spills and are easy to clean; some have porcelain burner caps that you can remove for cleaning.

Traditional electric coil burners avoid an open flame but take longer to heat up and cool down and are more difficult to clean than other types of burners.

Solid-disk electric burners have a solid, cast-iron cooking surface that's easier to clean than coils.

Ceramic glass cooktops feature special electric coils or halogen elements under an easy-to-clean, see-through ceramic glass cover. Halogen elements heat faster than coils but cost more. Cookware with thick, flat bottoms heats most efficiently on smooth cooktops.

Magnetic-induction cooktops are smooth and easy to clean. An electromagnetic field generates the heat. These models are sometimes called cool-tops because a ferrous-metal pan (i.e., steel, stainless steel, or cast iron), not the cooktop surface, cooks the food.

High-output and simmering burners on many ranges and cooktops give you power to boil big pots of water quickly or, on the other hand, use low, even heat for simmering sauces and melting chocolate.

Griddles and grills—available on many higher-priced ranges and cooktops—allow you to make bacon, eggs, and pancakes for a crowd or grill meat without having to use an outdoor appliance.

OVENS

Commercial, combination, and high-tech units offer more choices than ever before.

Traditional thermal ovens, gas or electric, use heat elements to roast, bake, and broil.

Convection ovens, available as an option on electric, gas, and dual-fuel ranges, use fans to circulate heated air around food for faster, more even cooking. Convection cooking bakes crustier breads, juicier roasts, and three racks of cookies at one time.

Combination units combine convection cooking with microwave power for faster cooking. Some add a broiling element to cook, brown, and crisp in one operation.

Convection steam ovens seal in nutrients, flavor, and color by injecting steam to cook most foods in 20 minutes or less. Steam cooking also defrosts and reheats food without sacrificing moisture or flavor.

Warming drawers that fit right into standard-size cabinets keep food hot and dinner plates warm.

Programmable refrigerating ovens cool the oven compartment for up to 24 hours and then heat up for cooking. The convenient programmable features let you set times and temperatures.

VENTS

You have a choice of updraft or downdraft ventilation systems.

Updraft systems have a hood that pulls air through a filter and along ductwork to the outside.

Downdraft systems either fit flush on a cooktop or rise above the countertop. These systems draw out air through ductwork under the floor.

Either way, look for a capacity that matches your cooktop and is as quiet a unit as you can find.

Vent fan capacity is rated by how many cubic feet of air per minute (cfm) a fan moves. If you cook on a conventional electric range, you need a fan rated at 200 cfm. For conventional gas ranges select a vent fan with a capacity of 200–300 cfm. If you do a lot of cooking on a professional- or semiprofessional-style gas range, you'll need up to 1,500 cfm.

Fan sound level is rated in sones. Lower numbers designate a quieter unit. One sone, for example, is similar to a humming refrigerator. Doubling the sone rating is the same as doubling the noise level of the appliance.

DISHWASHERS

Traditional models offer sleek, easy-clean, trimless fronts with touch-pad controls—some located at the top of the door to further disguise the appliance. Some accept panels to match cabinetry.

Special features abound, including adjustable-height racks, multiple cycle settings, and dirt sensors that adjust the water level based on the amount of soil. Extra-quiet motors and vibration-absorbing materials minimize noise level. High-capacity models have more room than traditional models; those with three racks ensure efficient use

of space. For large families or frequent entertaining, install two dishwashers.

Dishwasher drawers take up half the space of floor-to-counter models. Run only one to save water and energy when you have only a few dishes; with two, you can wash greasy pans in one and fine crystal in the other.

REFRIGERATORS

Though any functioning model will keep foods cold, decide whether a top freezer (typically the least expensive), bottom freezer, side-by-side, or built-in style (typically the most expensive) best meets your needs. Once you've determined the type, look for convenience features including:

Sealed and raised edges on glass shelves contain spills and make for easier cleaning.

Door-mounted icemakers, rather than those mounted inside the freezer cabinet, free up freezer space and make it easier to fill ice chests and buckets.

Undercounter icemakers produce up to 60 pounds of clear ice cubes a day for big families, frequent entertainers, or filling large coolers.

Climate-controlled compartments, which keep fruit, produce, and meat at their ideal temperature and humidity, extend storage life and prevent food from drying out or getting soggy.

Glass doors allow you to see what's inside when the door is closed, so you can take inventory without warming the contents.

Refrigerator drawers, similar to dishwasher drawers, come in 27- and 30-inch widths that can be customized with removable exterior panels to match cabinetry. These handy drawers store everything from soft drinks to fresh fruit.

Wine coolers keep wines at the perfect temperature for long storage and at the right humidity to prevent corks from drying out. Some models have three separate temperature zones for red, white, and sparkling wines.

Cabinetry

Cabinets often consume 40 percent of a new or completely remodeled kitchen's budget, so select yours carefully. Fortunately, manufactured cabinets have improved quality and offer an impressive list of standard features and furniturelike style formerly available only to custom buyers. Features that you can order with many stock and semicustom cabinets include recycling bin inserts, drawer dividers, bread savers, pasta bins, wine racks, appliance garages, file drawers, lazy Susans, and angled spice inserts. Furniturelike details include clear and decorative glass doors, footed base cabinets, fretwork, carved inlays, arched valances, and punched-tin door inserts. Turned legs make kitchen cabinetry that's reminiscent of fine period furniture. It's a detail that's especially attractive in homes that have open floor plans where the kitchen work core is on display to living and dining areas.

While you're selecting features and style, keep your eye out for quality. A little experience with cabinetry anatomy will help you make smart selections.

TYPES

Choose face-frame or frameless cabinet styles.

Face-frame cabinets attach framing to the front of the cabinet box. This type of construction is sturdy and stable and results in a more traditional look. Drawers and pullouts are somewhat smaller than the overall cabinet dimensions because they must fit within the framing. As a result, these cabinets offer less capacity than their frameless counterparts. The grain on good quality face-frame cabinets matches that of the drawers.

Frameless cabinets have door hinges that attach to the inside of the cabinet for a contemporary look. They have a somewhat larger capacity than

framed cabinets, but are more difficult to plan for and install because you must take into account door clearances and filler panels. These are needed when cabinets are installed at an angle to one another.

MATERIALS

Three materials form the support structure of most cabinets.

Particleboard serves as the base for most laminate and some veneered cabinets. Look for 45-pound commercial grade particleboard; poorer grades won't hold screws well.

Medium-density fiberboard (MDF) is a high-quality substrate material that offers a smooth surface and edges that you can shape and paint.

Plywood is the strongest of the materials and offers the best structural support.

JOINTS

Joints give cabinets their strength and stability; the better the joint, the better the cabinet.

Butt joints are the least sturdy option: The cabinet pieces are simply glued to each other.

Dado joints are more robust than butt joints. The sides fit into grooves cut into the cabinet back and the face frame.

Gussets are triangular braces glued into the upper corners of the cabinet boxes to add even more strength.

DRAWERS

Look for quality drawers that:

Glide smoothly on ball-bearing-equipped nylon wheels that roll on 75-pound capacity metal rails.

Extend fully so you have full access to the contents without removing the drawer from the cabinet.

Don't wobble when fully extended.

Close automatically if pulled out less than 1 inch on self-closing guides.

Have dovetail or dowel joints at the corners for long-term durability.

Are sturdily made of $1/2$- or $3/4$-inch solid wood sides and plywood bottom panels that are set into grooves.

CABINET FRONTS

Choose from the following kinds:

Full-inset fronts are flush with the cabinet frame. Because these require excellent craftsmanship, only custom cabinets feature them.

Partial-overlay fronts conceal the opening but reveal some of the frame. This style is affordable because it's easier to construct.

Full-overlay doors are the only option available for frameless cabinetry because they cover the entire box front. When used on face-frame cabinetry, a full overlay covers the entire frame.

DOORS

Most cabinet doors feature versatile frame-and-panel construction; custom cabinets often feature solid wood.

Frame-and-panel doors "float" a panel of solid wood, veneered panel, clear or patterned glass, or other material within the wood frame.

Solid-wood doors consist of several pieces of wood glued together for the appearance of one solid panel. For stability, manufacturers screw wood crosspieces to the back.

SHELVES AND TRAYS

The following three options help you organize cabinet space.

Shelves are best constructed from $3/4$-inch, 45-pound commercial-grade particleboard covered with a durable material, such as laminate or melamine.

Adjustable shelves are held in place with removable metal pins or plastic clips inserted into holes.

Roll-out trays make better use of space than shallow shelves, and the low sides provide easy access. Often subjected to heavier weight than drawers, roll-out trays require high-quality glides.

In a small kitchen, cabinet selection is particularly important to maximize space and good looks. Cabinets in this angled kitchen include spots for wine, the microwave oven, and a television.

Countertops

Countertops are an important feature of any kitchen. A dizzying array of materials makes for innumerable options, from standard laminate to contemporary concrete. Choose just one of these materials for your kitchen or use two or more to customize work areas and attractively break up long surfaces. You might, for example, set a stone slab in the baking area for rolling dough and another material on the perimeter cabinetry. Generally stone, faux-stone, concrete, and stainless steel prove most expensive; laminate is generally the least expensive. Cost varies widely, however, depending upon region, pattern, and installation.

Ceramic tile handles hot pans without scorching, is moisture-resistant, and comes in a host of colors, patterns, and textures, making the decorative possibilities infinite—think geometric designs, borders, and mosaics. But it can crack or chip if struck with a heavy object. The tiles themselves wipe clean with a damp cloth, but surrounding grout joints sometimes stain. To minimize discoloration, install a tiled countertop using narrow grout joints, epoxy grout, or even a darker color grout.

Concrete is an increasingly popular option that complements a variety of kitchen aesthetics. It may be gray or dyed and inlaid with other elements to create custom looks. The material must be sealed regularly and stands up well under heat, but it still is subject to stains. Three techniques are used to install concrete countertops: First, you can order concrete tiles and concrete slabs from home improvement centers and install them on-site. (If desired, you can have them colored before they're installed.) Second, you can have site-poured counters built by a contractor. Forms are built on top of cabinets, and then filled with concrete. Finally, you can install site-poured counters that require metal forms that remain in place, adding a contrasting gleaming edge to the grainy material. The price of a concrete counter is somewhat less than stone and about the same as stainless steel.

Engineered quartz has an appearance, composition, weight, and price that are all comparable to granite. Made of quartz that's bound together with space-age polymers, it captures the crystalline sparkle and density of granite, but is nonporous so it does not require sealing and is less susceptible to stains. Manufacturers claim that it's tougher than granite and less susceptible to chipping and cracking.

Granite is prized for its natural beauty and durability, whether polished to a high gloss or honed to a matte finish. Its variegated, crystalline structure makes for a lively play of light on its surface. Granite is ultrasmooth and cool, providing a suitable surface for kneading and rolling dough. On the downside, it requires periodic treatment with a nontoxic penetrating sealant to keep its surface in top condition, and a sharp blow with a pointed object can chip it. Solid granite is expensive; for a lower cost option, consider granite tiles.

Laminate, an affordable, durable, low-maintenance surface, offers a tremendous range of colors, patterns, and textures, some of which look like more expensive, natural materials. While laminate stands up to grease and stains and wipes clean with soap and water, it's vulnerable to sharp knives and hot pans. Heavy blows can dent the surface, and prolonged exposure to water may dissolve glue lines and cause the subsurface to warp. Better grades of laminate feature color throughout the material, making scratches and chips less visible. You can buy laminate countertop sections finished with a variety of front edge treatments, with or without attached backsplashes.

Marble, like granite, has a cool-to-the-touch surface that makes it ideal for baking and making candy, but it is much softer and more porous than granite. It sometimes fractures along veining; offers less resistance to stains, scratches, and general wear; and must be sealed often.

1: Mixing countertop materials creates ideal surfaces for different kitchen tasks. Here the island top mixes marble—a cool surface good for rolling out dough—with a section of butcher block perfect for prep work.

2: Black granite countertops are studded with quartz chips that catch the light and add subtle color variation.

3: Granite countertops are gorgeous, nearly indestructible and are available in a wide variety of colors and grain patterns. Even in light tones granite is less likely to stain than more porous stones such as marble and limestone.

4: Tile countertops—especially those with light-color grout—require care to avoid grout stains but make an ideal surface around the cooktop because the tiles will handle hot-from-the-stove pots and pans.

Soapstone, a traditional choice for old-fashioned sinks, has a mellow luster, velvety feel, and muted gray-green color. Soapstone is stain- and heat-resistant and durable, but it's also soft, needs to be sealed, and distresses to a patina over years of use.

Solid-surfacing, made of plastic resin composites, comes in a variety of thicknesses. A wide range of colors, patterns, and natural-material look-alikes is available. The material is also known for its design flexibility, allowing the creation of special effects through inlays of contrasting colors. Because color runs through the material, nicks are camouflaged. The nonporous material resists stains but does scratch and scorch. Minor damage sands out.

Stainless steel is popular for creating commercial-style kitchens. It is also the only material besides solid-surfacing that allows one-piece countertop/sink formations, eliminating the dirt-catching seam between the counter and the sink bowl. Stainless steel withstands hot pots and pans and is easy to clean. It does scratch, though, so you can't use it for a cutting surface. Surface finishes range from a mirrorlike gleam to a matte glow; you can also opt for lightly brushed, relief-stamped, or embossed. The shinier the surface, the more noticeable fingerprints and marks.

Sinks and Faucets

Most kitchen chores involve the sink, so choose a bowl and faucet that are versatile and durable.

SINK MATERIALS
A variety of metals, natural materials, and faux-natural materials is available for sinks.

Stainless steel is the most popular choice: It's durable and lightweight, making it easy to install. Thickness and finish contribute to quality. A thick 19-gauge sink won't dent easily, a nickel-and-stainless composition wards off water spots, and a brushed finish—rather than a mirror finish—conceals scratches. Stainless-steel sinks are among the least expensive sink options, although restaurant-quality, one-piece stainless sink-and-counter combinations can be pricey.

Enameled cast-iron sinks perform well and provide the kitchen with an extra shot of color—especially those that have apron fronts, which expose the front of the sink. These sinks are extremely durable. They are more expensive than stainless-steel sinks, less forgiving of dropped glassware and china than stainless-steel, and because they're quite heavy, can be difficult to install.

Vitreous china is easy to clean, colorful, and attractive, but it is also susceptible to chipping.

Quartz composite resists scratches and stains, and the wide range of colors and grains looks great with stone countertops.

Solid-surface materials offer many color choices as well as stone look-alikes. One-piece, integrated sinks and countertops are available for a seamless look and easy cleaning.

Soapstone sinks are experiencing a comeback as people rediscover their muted, green-gray tones, solid feel, and soft patina.

Copper offers a rich color accent, but eventually oxidizes to a gray-green color unless polished regularly. Because copper is soft, these sinks easily dent.

SINK TYPES
The type you choose largely depends on your countertop material.

Self-rimming sinks—the most common variety—are the easiest to install. With a rim that overlays the countertop, these retrofit into existing countertops (as long as the opening is the same size). They also protect laminate countertops from moisture damage. Although debris collects around the sink rim, it is easy to clean.

Undermount sinks mount to the bottom of a stone or solid-surface countertop, emphasizing countertop material and making cleanup easy because you can sweep crumbs directly from the counter into the sink. You generally can't use them with laminate countertops because they expose the counter substrate. Both sink and countertop require expert installation.

1: An undermount stainless-steel sink—paired with sleek granite countertops—is perfectly suited to this contemporary kitchen. Undermount sinks are great for showing off the full thickness of counters made from natural or engineered stone or solid-surfacing.

2: Farmhouse sinks lend a vintage air to the kitchen. If you like the style but want the convenience of a double-bowl sink, consider positioning two farmhouse sinks adjacent to each other; or if space allows, install a separate prep sink near the cooking area.

3: Pot-filler faucets are convenient when located on the backsplash at the range. They prevent the cook from carrying a heavy pot filled with water across the room. Locate pot-fillers high enough above the cooktop so large pots easily fit under the faucet.

Integrated bowl sinks and countertops are made of one seamless material for a flawless look and easy cleanup. Material options are limited to higher-cost stainless and solid-surface products.

SINK CONFIGURATIONS AND OPTIONS

It used to be simple: one bowl or two. Now choose from several options:

Single-bowl sinks are ideal for soaking big pots and pans.

Double-bowl sinks handle food preparation and dish-soaking simultaneously.

Triple-bowl sinks add a center-well disposer.

L-shape sinks in either double- or triple-bowl configurations are good for corner locations in kitchens with limited counter space.

Extra-deep bowls—some as deep as 14 inches—are useful for filling tall pots and washing large quantities of dishes and cookware.

Fitted cutting boards partially cover one basin, freeing up counter space.

FAUCETS

While the sink category can be broken down into a few materials and types, the same can't be said for faucets. Brushed and polished chrome are still staples, but brass, powder-coated epoxy in bright colors, and even gold-plate faucets have joined the mix. Reproduction and vintage-look styles are available, as is a range of contemporary designs.

Commercial faucets and accessories, such as pot-fillers that rise to fill large containers and high-capacity sprayers, are now available for home use. Even conventional residential faucets are versatile, with scraper-spray and brush-spray combinations or pullout wands that change from stream to spray. Washerless and ceramic disk valves have replaced leaky rubber washers. Antiscald faucets protect children from hot-water burns, and integrated purified water dispensers eliminate the need to buy bottled water.

Flooring

As you prepare and serve meals, you're on your feet in the kitchen a lot. That's why flooring is important. Base your selection on a balance of comfort, maintenance, durability, and good looks. Here's a sampling of what's available.

BAMBOO

This durable, eco-friendly choice looks like hardwood (it's actually three layers of grass laminated under high pressure to create planks). Multiple coats of acrylic urethane make the surface durable and resistant to water, mildew, and insect damage. Harder than maple and oak, bamboo also expands and contracts less. Because bamboo plants (not the kind eaten by pandas) produce new shoots, it's an easily sustainable product. Bamboo flooring comes unfinished or finished, and you can glue or nail it to a subfloor.

CERAMIC TILE

A variety of sizes and colors allows you to create patterns with tile. Tiles are available both glazed and unglazed; a glazed finish is a good choice for kitchens because it prevents moisture from soaking in, although high-traffic areas with glazed tiles may eventually show some wear. Ceramic tile is durable, resistant to moisture, and generally low-maintenance. On the downside, ceramic tile often feels cold, is unforgiving when you drop glassware, and can be difficult to stand on for long periods of time. Further, food and dirt collect in the grout lines.

CORK

This resilient, cushioned surface is quiet underfoot, comfortable, and moisture-resistant. Made from renewable bark harvested from cork trees in Mediterranean forests, it requires a urethane finish for easy sweeping and mopping. Cork comes in tiles or planks, which allow for easy repair should damage occur. Installation is similar to vinyl tile. This type of flooring can last for decades when cared for correctly: Every few years you must sand the old finish and reapply new urethane.

HARDWOOD

A good option to bring warmth and classic good looks to a kitchen. It's available in many species; in solid, engineered, or parquet form; and it is sold prefinished or unfinished. Solid planks can be sanded and refinished many times. Engineered planks consist of two or more layers of wood laminated together (a hardwood veneer "wear" layer and lower layers of softwood). Because the wear layer is relatively thin, you cannot continually refinish. Generally solid wood floors are site-finished, whereas engineered wood floors are prefinished. In both cases new clear finishes are tougher and more durable and water-resistant than ever, although wood may still be susceptible to water damage in high-traffic areas.

LAMINATES

Get the look of wood, tile, stone, or other natural materials at a comparably lower price. Early-generation laminates required installers to glue planks together, a tedious process that sometimes resulted in failed joints and moisture damage. Laminates now snap together, cutting installation time and resulting in tighter, more even, watertight joints. Note that some laminate products are not recommended for use in areas exposed to high humidity, and most manufacturers recommend mopping up standing water promptly. Available in squares, strips, or rectangles, laminate is durable and easy to clean, and requires little maintenance. Keep in mind that it can't be refinished or restained like wood.

LINOLEUM

Made primarily of natural materials, linoleum has made a comeback. It's made of natural linseed oil, resin, cork, limestone, and wood flour mixed with pigments, then rolled onto a jute backing and dried. Soft underfoot, it comes in both tiles and sheets of solid or flecked colors and is easy to care for. As the linseed oil dries, it actually becomes harder and more durable than vinyl. Although old-style linoleum tended to fade, today's linoleum offers bright, lasting color.

STONE

Harder varieties, notably granite, require little maintenance and are nearly indestructible. Others, such as marble and limestone, are more porous, stain easily, and require more maintenance.

2

Some varieties—such as slate—crack and chip. Stone is cold, hard, and unforgiving. Professional installation often is required.

VINYL

A low-cost and easy-care choice, vinyl is available in sheets and tiles. You'll find a wide selection of colors and styles, including stone, tile, and hardwood look-alikes. Some tiles come in easy-to-install, self-adhesive form, although they tend to eventually loosen and admit moisture and dirt. Less-expensive vinyl may puncture, fade, and discolor, whereas good-quality, higher-cost sheet vinyl looks good, is easy to maintain, and lasts for many years.

1: Resilient cork floors provide a cushioned surface. Though the material is enjoying current popular attention, it's a natural in this Victorian-era home that originally featured an 1890s floor made from linseed and cork.

2: Dark quartersawn oak plank floors are a dramatic contrast to the lighthearted green cabinetry in this Georgian-style home.

Lighting

Lighting is a major tool for making your kitchen livable and inviting. When planning a lighting scheme, don't think only of electrical fixtures: Windows that bring in great views and large doses of sunshine are great sources of light. Weigh storage needs with your desire for more natural light, and you may decide to sacrifice a few upper cabinets for more windows. To keep your kitchen bright, keep the following lighting basics in mind.

General, or ambient, lighting radiates a comfortable level of brightness throughout a room. A room is usually more pleasing when the general lighting comes from a blend of sources. In smaller kitchens (less than 120 square feet), you could center one ceiling-mounted fixture (use two or more for larger kitchens) and add recessed spotlights to the perimeter. Or you can use perimeter soffit lights that direct light upward to reflect off the ceiling. As a guideline, provide at least 100 watts of incandescent light or 25 watts of fluorescent light for each 50 square feet of floor space.

Task lighting illuminates a specific area, such as a sink, cleanup center, or food preparation area. Its purpose is to prevent eyestrain, and you can create it with undercabinet lights as well as ceiling- or wall-mounted fixtures. Generally you should provide each work center with a minimum of 100 to 150 watts of incandescent light or 25 to 35 watts of fluorescent light. When used for undercabinet lighting, fluorescent tubes should extend along two-thirds of the length of the counter they light and provide about 8 watts of power per lineal foot of counter.

Accent lighting spotlights the best features of your room. Track, recessed, or wall-mounted fixtures—often equipped with the focused, bright-white beam of a halogen light—provide accent illumination. Designers make it a point to include beautiful indirect lighting techniques behind glass-fronted cabinets, over the tops of cabinetry, bouncing off the ceiling, and tucked into cabinet toe-kicks to show off flooring.

BULBS

The types of lightbulbs available have increased. Whether you're building or remodeling a kitchen, now is a great time to rethink what's supplying your artificial light.

Incandescent bulbs are traditionally used for most household illumination. They're inexpensive, but they don't last particularly long. Most of the energy they consume produces heat, not light, making them energy inefficient and adding to the load on your cooling system during warm weather. They're a good choice for lights that are rarely used because their initial cost is low.

Energy-efficient bulbs are incandescents that typically use 5 to 13 percent less energy than traditional incandescents with a minimal reduction in light output. They cost slightly more but recoup the difference in energy savings over the course of their lives. These bulbs are great for moderate-use fixtures or for anyone who has an aversion to fluorescent light.

Halogen bulbs are more efficient than incandescents and last three to four times longer. These are great for track and spotlights because you can use a lower wattage bulb and get the same illumination as larger-watt incandescents. Some halogen lights have the added advantage of being small and can produce a very concentrated white light, making them ideal for highly directional accent lighting.

Retrofit and compact fluorescent lights screw into the same sockets as incandescents but use about 75 percent less energy and last 10 times longer. Although they cost more, they save many times the purchase price in energy over the course of their lives. Because they last so long, they're a great choice for hard-to-access fixtures. They're available in light outputs that correspond to most incandescent bulbs.

Linear fluorescent lights are the familiar fluorescent tubes that have been lighting kitchens for decades. They're a great choice for illuminating large spaces with even, glare-free, shadow-free illumination.

1: The light fixtures above this island provide effective task lighting and offer overall ambient lighting for the kitchen. Lights under the range hood provide bright light for the cooktop.

2: Pendent lights provide task lighting above islands and countertops. A wide variety of styles and finishes is available. Some hang from tracks, allowing you to change their placement.

3: Windows are an important component of any kitchen lighting scheme, allowing natural light to enter the room. Positioning new windows in the same locations as those they are replacing will cut remodeling costs.

Now that you're familiar with the options available for making your kitchen more efficient and attractive, this chapter offers additional insights—including a kitchen remodeling checklist and a breakdown of the various types of kitchen configurations—to help you launch your dream, as well as an extensive list of resources and contact information to help you turn it into a beautiful reality.

strategies

Wish List

Planning the kitchen you want requires that you first understand the kitchen you have. Then you need to think about what you'd like to change and how you'd change it.

This checklist will help you identify the advantages and disadvantages of the kitchen you're living with now, what your needs are, and what you'd like to have in your new kitchen.

> Use this list to identify the features of your current kitchen that you want to change when you build or remodel. First check those items that are problems in your current kitchen. Then, for each checked item, prioritize your kitchen project with the following number system: 1 = must fix, 2 = want to fix, 3 = would be nice to fix, but can live with it.

First evaluate the kitchen you have now using the kitchen evaluation checklist to consider how the higher-priority problems may be corrected in a renovation, or avoided altogether with a new kitchen.

Then work your way through the checklist on the opposite page. Note how you use your current kitchen and how you'd like to use your new or remodeled one.

With your prioritized kitchen uses in mind, continue through the questionnaire, noting what storage needs, work centers, and appliances your new or remodeled kitchen will have.

Refer to this checklist as you continue to plan your kitchen and take it with you when you talk to kitchen designers, architects, or contractors.

KITCHEN EVALUATION

	Problem	Priority (1, 2, 3)
Traffic		
Do entries impede the work core?	O	_____
Does the table block entries?	O	_____
Does traffic interrupt cooking?	O	_____
Are other traffic problems apparent?	O	_____
Cooking		
When preparing meals, are you cut off from others?	O	_____
Do you need workstations for multiple cooks?	O	_____
Are there too many steps between appliances and the sink?	O	_____
Is ample counterspace lacking beside the cooktop and refrigerator?	O	_____
Does your kitchen fail to meet the needs of special cooking interests?	O	_____
Cleanup		
Is the dishwasher far from the sink?	O	_____
Should the table be closer to the sink and dishwasher?	O	
Could you benefit from a second dishwasher?	O	_____
Do you need a place for recyclables or garbage?	O	_____
Storage		
Are your cabinets crowded?	O	_____
Would you benefit from a walk-in pantry or a pantry cabinet?	O	_____
Are your existing refrigerator and freezer too small?	O	_____
Surfaces		
Are you dissatisfied with the current surfaces?	O	_____
Are the surfaces difficult to clean?	O	_____
Is the flooring uncomfortable or worn?	O	_____
Light and Views		
Is your kitchen shadowy?	O	_____
Do you want views from the sink and the range?	O	_____
Dining		
Do you need a place for dining in the kitchen?	O	_____
Do you encounter seating difficulties when you entertain?	O	_____

PROJECT CHECKLIST

Use this list to determine how you use your kitchen, how you'd like to use your kitchen, and what appliances and fixtures you have or need. Then prioritize the items you checked using the following number system: 1 = must have, 2 = want to have, 3 = would be nice to have, but can do without.

	Current Kitchen	New Kitchen	Priority (1, 2, 3)		Current Kitchen	New Kitchen	Priority (1, 2, 3)
Kitchen Uses				Electric crockery cooker	[ ]	[ ]	_____
Computing	[ ]	[ ]	_____	Electric dehydrator	[ ]	[ ]	_____
Entertaining	[ ]	[ ]	_____	Electric grill	[ ]	[ ]	_____
Family cooking	[ ]	[ ]	_____	Electric juicer	[ ]	[ ]	_____
Gourmet cooking	[ ]	[ ]	_____	Electric knife sharpener	[ ]	[ ]	_____
Homework	[ ]	[ ]	_____	Electric wok	[ ]	[ ]	_____
Laundry	[ ]	[ ]	_____	Espresso maker	[ ]	[ ]	_____
TV viewing	[ ]	[ ]	_____	Flour/grain mill	[ ]	[ ]	_____
				Food processor	[ ]	[ ]	_____
Storage				Ice cream maker	[ ]	[ ]	_____
Cleaning products	[ ]	[ ]	_____	Meat grinder	[ ]	[ ]	_____
Food	[ ]	[ ]	_____	Mixer, hand	[ ]	[ ]	_____
Linens	[ ]	[ ]	_____	Mixer, stand	[ ]	[ ]	_____
Separate butler's pantry	[ ]	[ ]	_____	Pasta machine	[ ]	[ ]	_____
Shelves	[ ]	[ ]	_____	Popcorn popper	[ ]	[ ]	_____
Small appliances	[ ]	[ ]	_____	Rice cooker	[ ]	[ ]	_____
Specialty dishes	[ ]	[ ]	_____	Toaster	[ ]	[ ]	_____
Standard dishes	[ ]	[ ]	_____	Toaster oven	[ ]	[ ]	_____
Utensils	[ ]	[ ]	_____	Yogurt maker	[ ]	[ ]	_____
Work Centers							
Cleanup	[ ]	[ ]	_____	**Large Appliances**			
Cooking	[ ]	[ ]	_____	Cooktop	[ ]	[ ]	_____
Food prep	[ ]	[ ]	_____	Dishwasher	[ ]	[ ]	_____
Food storage	[ ]	[ ]	_____	Dishwasher drawers	[ ]	[ ]	_____
Formal dining	[ ]	[ ]	_____	Dishwasher, second	[ ]	[ ]	_____
Informal dining	[ ]	[ ]	_____	Disposer	[ ]	[ ]	_____
Planning	[ ]	[ ]	_____	Freezer	[ ]	[ ]	_____
Sink, single-bowl	[ ]	[ ]	_____	Oven, combination	[ ]	[ ]	_____
Sink, double-bowl	[ ]	[ ]	_____	Oven, convection	[ ]	[ ]	_____
Sink, triple-bowl	[ ]	[ ]	_____	Oven, conventional	[ ]	[ ]	_____
Sink, secondary prep	[ ]	[ ]	_____	Oven, dual-fuel	[ ]	[ ]	_____
Specialty	[ ]	[ ]	_____	Oven, microwave	[ ]	[ ]	_____
				Range, freestanding	[ ]	[ ]	_____
Small Appliances				Refrigerator	[ ]	[ ]	_____
Baby-food maker	[ ]	[ ]	_____	Refrigerator drawers	[ ]	[ ]	_____
Blender	[ ]	[ ]	_____	Trash compactor	[ ]	[ ]	_____
Bread machine	[ ]	[ ]	_____	Vent, downdraft	[ ]	[ ]	_____
Cappuccino maker	[ ]	[ ]	_____	Vent, overhead	[ ]	[ ]	_____
Coffee grinder	[ ]	[ ]	_____	Warming drawers	[ ]	[ ]	_____
Coffeemaker	[ ]	[ ]	_____	Washer/dryer	[ ]	[ ]	_____
Deep fat fryer	[ ]	[ ]	_____	Water purifier	[ ]	[ ]	_____
Electric can opener	[ ]	[ ]	_____	Wine cooler	[ ]	[ ]	_____

Kitchen Configurations

Kitchens come in all shapes and sizes. The kitchen layout that will be most efficient and aesthetically pleasing to you—and most feasible in the space with which you have to work—depends on the dimensions of your kitchen, the basic shape the walls make, how you want your kitchen to relate to the spaces that surround it, and whether you want to create informal dining space within the kitchen proper.

Each layout presented here has its strong and weak points. Consider these shapes an excellent place to start—then manipulate them to suit your needs.

THE WORK TRIANGLE

No matter what layout you choose, keep your eye on the work triangle. This is the triangle that's formed by drawing lines from the sink to the refrigerator to the cooktop. A nice, tight work triangle is the key to an efficient kitchen. If the distance between the three features it connects is more than a few steps, you will likely tire as you rush here and there to prepare, cook, and clean.

If more than one cook will use your kitchen at the same time, plot the elements so traffic flows smoothly. Adding a second sink and cooktop so each cook has his or her own area creates two triangles that intersect only at one point, for instance, the refrigerator.

Professional kitchen planners often talk about "work zones" and "work centers" in addition to or instead of work triangles, but the concept is the same: Keep the elements you need grouped together to avoid wasted steps and plot traffic routes so that stoplights aren't needed to avoid collisions.

KITCHEN SHAPES

One-Wall. This layout is the least efficient because it places the range, refrigerator, sink, and storage along one wall. These kitchens work best with a centered sink flanked by refrigerator and cooktop, with 4 feet of counterspace between each. Place doors away from the busy work wall to avoid traffic hassles.

U-Shape

G-Shape

Galley

L-Shape
with Island

L-Shape

One-Wall

This U-shape kitchen is a textbook example of an efficient work core with the cooktop, sink, and refrigerator all within a couple of convenient footsteps from one another.

Galley. Many older homes have this type of long, narrow kitchen built between parallel walls. Galley kitchens are incredibly efficient work spaces. They allow the cook to move easily with few steps between the sink, refrigerator, stove, and work spaces. Plan at least 4 feet of space between opposite counters. The best design puts the sink and the refrigerator on one wall, with the cooktop centered between them on the opposite wall. Unfortunately a galley kitchen doesn't allow for much dining space, although some longer galleys successfully incorporate a breakfast nook at one end.

L-Shape. This layout requires two adjacent walls and is most efficient when work areas are kept close to the crook of the L. You can save footsteps by routing the traffic flow from refrigerator to sink to cooktop to serving areas. Because the work core tucks into a corner, traffic through the kitchen isn't a problem.

L-Shape with Island. Adding an island to the L-shape kitchen makes room for more than one cook and adds counterspace, a place for a snack or breakfast bar, and increased space for storage and dining. The island also works as a room divider, shielding kitchen clutter from adjacent spaces.

U-Shape. The cozy U-shape kitchen works best when it places one workstation—the sink, cooktop, and refrigerator—on each of the three walls. The U-shape kitchen is highly efficient for one cook and allows for many design possibilities, but you need at least an 8×8-foot space to make it work. A small U-shape makes it difficult for multiple cooks to maneuver without getting in one another's way.

U-Shape with Island. If you're not sure how to make your large kitchen work efficiently, this layout may be the answer. You can install a sink or cooktop in the island and, if desired, a special function countertop such as marble or granite for rolling pastry. Allow at least 42 inches of aisle space to surround the island; if yours is a two-cook kitchen, 48 inches is better.

G-Shape. This layout features a peninsula anchored to a line of cabinets. You can outfit the peninsula with a cooktop or sink, enabling you to face guests while working, or you can use the peninsula as a dining bar or buffet. The peninsula also serves as a room divider, allowing family and friends to visit with the cook while remaining clear of the work area.

1: A compact work area makes this small kitchen efficient. Dishwasher drawers are located at one side of the sink and refrigerator drawers are on the other, across from the range.

2: L-shape-with-island kitchens offer galleylike efficiency and more. The island serves as a work space, a storage unit, a dining and serving counter, and a divider that keeps guests near, yet clear of the work core.

1

Kitchen Zones

Interrelated centers, or zones, make your kitchen more organized, efficient, and comfortable. Just as the work triangle puts the refrigerator, sink, and cooktop within easy reach, work centers with specific functions make planning, preparing, cooking, serving, and cleaning up after a meal quick and easy. Here's an overview of the different kitchen centers and some things to keep in mind as you design them.

Planning. Reserving a space in the kitchen to plan meals, leave and collect messages, pay bills, and use a computer is a necessity for many homeowners. Locate the planning center well outside any work traffic or access to storage cabinetry or appliances. If possible, include storage for books, files, a computer, and peripherals.

Cleanup. This center consists of the sink, garbage disposer, dishwasher, trash can or compactor, and a recycling bin. The sink anchors this zone and is best located in the center of the work triangle, between the range and the refrigerator. The dishwasher belongs next to the sink to the left if the main user is right-handed and to the right if that person is left-handed. If your plans include a trash compactor, install it on the side of the sink opposite the dishwasher to save steps. The cleanup center also requires a dish draining area and ample storage for dish towels, cleaning products, and utensils.

Food storage and prep. Here's where you'll put the refrigerator, well-organized storage for canned and dry goods, mixing bowls, cookware, cookbooks (if they're not stored in the planning center), and small appliances. Situate primary food storage near the longest stretch of countertop for easy access while cooking. It's best if those cabinets are attached to cool

1: This butler's pantry includes a coffee center complete with espresso maker and space for prepping a morning snack.
2: To make this cooking center efficient, frequently used utensils are stored on a wall-mounted system along the backsplash.

outside walls near shaded, north-facing windows and away from heat sources, such as the dishwasher or oven.

Cooking. The main ingredients here are the range (or cooktop and oven), its ventilation system, and a microwave oven. The cooking center also requires handy, accessible storage for all the tools of the cooking trade: pot holders, hot pads, spices and seasonings, and any other food products that go directly from the container into the simmering pot. If you imagined your new kitchen with a pot or utensil rack, put it here. Ideally, the cooking center should feature a heat-resistant surface near the range so you can remove hot pots from the heat without scorching the countertop. Can't find room for everything? Because baking doesn't require the close attention of stove-top cooking, consider placing ovens just outside the work triangle.

Serving and dining. Eat-in kitchens come with lots of advantages: They save steps when serving and cleaning up after a meal and provide family members and guests a place to talk, do

homework, or socialize with the cook. The ideal kitchen dining area enjoys close proximity to the work core and plenty of natural light. In small kitchens, the easiest way to gain dining space is to move all appliances to a galley or L-shape layout, leaving one wall or corner for a freestanding table and chairs or a built-in banquette. In a large kitchen, an island or peninsula with stools does the trick.

Specialty. If you have the space and the inclination, you can add centers designed to support other activities as well. If you're a baker, for instance, you might enjoy a baking center outfitted with a special surface for rolling dough and custom-designed storage for mixing bowls, baking pans, small appliances, oven mitts, and ingredients. If you entertain frequently, host numerous houseguests, or have a large family, a beverage center located outside the central work zones allows people to help themselves without entering the main kitchen. Other specialized centers might cater to snacking, recycling, or pet feeding.

1: To make this cooking center
   as efficient as possible,
   a nearby cabinet houses
   recessed shelves for large
   cooking oils and spice racks
   inside upper cabinet doors.
2: An adaptable island rolls
   wherever it's needed. Here
   it expands the baking center.
   The heavy mixer slides into the
   appliance garage when it's not
   in use.

Designing Your Kitchen

1

Now that you've composed your kitchen wish list and considered the variety of kitchen configurations and work centers, you're ready for the design.

DESIGNER OPTIONS

With so many options for kitchen plans, it can be tough getting started. Good thing there are lots of folks out there who can help.

Design it yourself. Using the Kitchen Planning Kit on pages 180–183, sketch out your space, mark the location of existing features, and experiment with different options. You may well want or need to consult a professional, but the exercise of working through options yourself will help clarify your priorities.

Get home center design help. Many home improvement centers employ staff who can help you lay out a kitchen at little or no charge. If you'll be working with stock cabinets and appliances, these folks often are great resources, streamlining both the design and product selection process. Keep in mind that you'll be responsible for supplying accurate measurements and you may not receive assistance with customizing or problem solving.

Hire a kitchen designer. Kitchens are such complex rooms that an entire profession is devoted to their design. Kitchen designers combine knowledge of interior design with an emphasis on kitchen use. They're also up-to-date on new and emerging kitchen products and technology. Certified Kitchen Designers have completed a course of study designed by the National Kitchen and Bath Association.

Consult an interior designer. Most interior designers address kitchens as well as other rooms. If you're remodeling more than your kitchen, you might choose an interior designer to assist you in pulling together the look of the entire project.

Commission an architect. Architects are especially valuable resources when you plan to make significant structural changes to your home, such as building a kitchen addition or substantially reworking its internal structure. They often work with interior designers and kitchen designers.

VISUALIZE YOUR KITCHEN

Once you have a preliminary design in hand, use these tips to visualize your new space and make the design work better for you.

Ask your architect or designer for a rendering. These three-dimensional color drawings, complete with furnishings, architectural features, and lighting sketched in, make it easier to get a feel for the prospective space.

Take a virtual tour. Your design pro might offer to let you "tour" your project before it's constructed using a computer-aided design (CAD) program. This software lets you experiment with configurations and view the space in three dimensions from different vantage points.

Stake it out. Outline the shape and size of your reconfigured room—especially if you're working on a major remodeling project or addition—using stake and string in the yard. If you're considering an addition, stake it out in the proposed final location. If you're considering a kitchen that uses existing space within the house, it's still useful to stake it out; just do it where you have sufficient room (for example, in your yard, garage, or driveway). Use objects such as lawn furniture and cardboard boxes to represent a dining set, cabinetry, and appliances within the staked-out area. Walk around the "room" and see how it feels.

SEAMLESS ADDITIONS

If your kitchen renovation involves an addition, blend it seamlessly with the

1: Remodeling this beautiful kitchen in a vintage home involved knocking down walls and carving out space for a larger cooking area. This kind of major renovation benefits from design and architectural expertise, ensuring the space functions well, integrates with the rest of the home, and meets building codes.

2: To accommodate the homeowner—a culinary school graduate who entertains for groups of 60 guests and who stands barely 5 feet 2 inches—this kitchen was carefully designed to make food preparation convenient. Countertops were installed at lower than standard height, and large undermount stainless-steel sinks are each a foot deep to accommodate oversize stock pots.

3: Working with a professional to design your kitchen should result in a space that suits your particular needs and style. This kitchen was fashioned to reflect the homeowner's desire for views of her garden, love of entertaining, and interest in understated French style.

rest of the home. Details make all the difference, so pay attention to three crucial factors: roofline, proportion, and materials.

Start at the top. Make sure all roof proportions mirror one another in style. Match the pitch, overhangs, soffits, fasciae, and eaves with the existing structure.

Maintain proportion. Take care that your kitchen addition won't overwhelm—or be overwhelmed by—the existing structure.

Choose materials carefully. On the roof, match shingle style, color, and material; when using brick, match its color, size, texture, and mortar to the original. Or complement the existing materials with something consistent with the period of the house. Windows too need to match, both in basic type and the details, such as muntin width and pane size. Lastly, choose a color palette in keeping with the home's period, style, and surroundings.

Kitchen Planning Kit

Consider all the details to transform your kitchen dreams into a reality. Few homeowners resist the urge to sketch out some ideas, even if they plan to work with a kitchen designer. Doing so is recommended because your drawings provide insight into what you're after.

Use the Kitchen Planning Kit on the following pages to work through the process. Visualize the following:
- ideal traffic flow
- placement of various work centers
- space for a planning area
- transitions from the kitchen to the rooms around it
- whether you'd like to incorporate a gathering, snacking, or dining area
- the types, sizes, and styles of appliances, cabinetry, shelving, and furnishings.

Plot the space using the grid on page 183 (1 square equals 1 square foot of floor space). Plot your kitchen, including any pantry, entry, mudroom, office, dining area, or bump-outs you'd like to add or remodel at the same time. One of the keys to making your kitchen both functional and beautiful is good placement of doors, windows, appliances, cabinetry, islands, and built-in features.

Use the following architectural symbols to mark the position of existing architectural features. Choose a different color to indicate added features such as the placement of built-ins and furniture. Draw dotted lines to mark obstructions, including prominent light fixtures and angled ceilings.

The templates offer the option to experiment with different placements for furniture, appliances, and built-in features. Trace or photocopy the appropriate items from the templates and cut them out with a crafts knife or scissors. If you have furniture or special features such as a peninsula or island, measure and draw them to the same scale (1 square equals 1 square foot) on the grid paper.

TEMPLATE TIME

Mark the placement of common kitchen components on your grid. The templates include both plan-view ("top-bottom") and elevation ("side view") perspectives, allowing you to create both floor plans and wall elevations. Most kitchen components are represented here, including various types and sizes of drop-in and freestanding ranges, cooktops, grills, and refrigerators. Pay attention to details like door swings and drawer extensions (marked in dotted lines on these templates) as you consider the placement of these items in the room. If you don't see a template for something you'd like to include, draw your own.

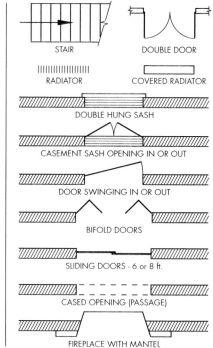

Base Cabinets

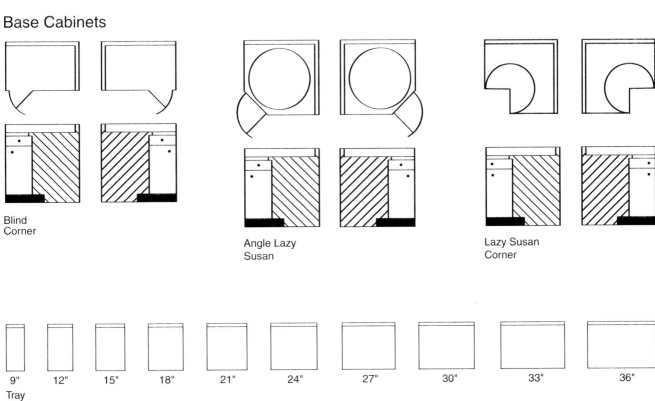

Blind Corner

Angle Lazy Susan

Lazy Susan Corner

9" Tray   12"   15"   18"   21"   24"   27"   30"   33"   36"

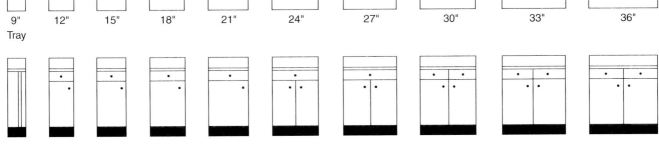

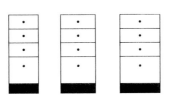

Sink Bases

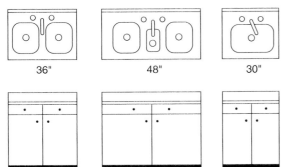

36"   48"   30"

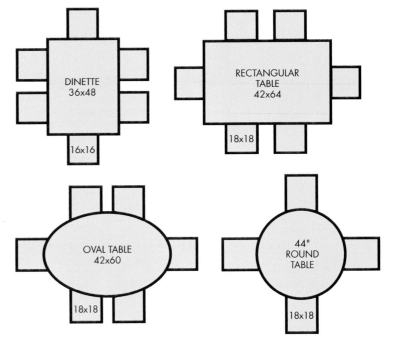

DINETTE
36x48

16x16

RECTANGULAR
TABLE
42x64

18x18

OVAL TABLE
42x60

18x18

44"
ROUND
TABLE

18x18

Appliances

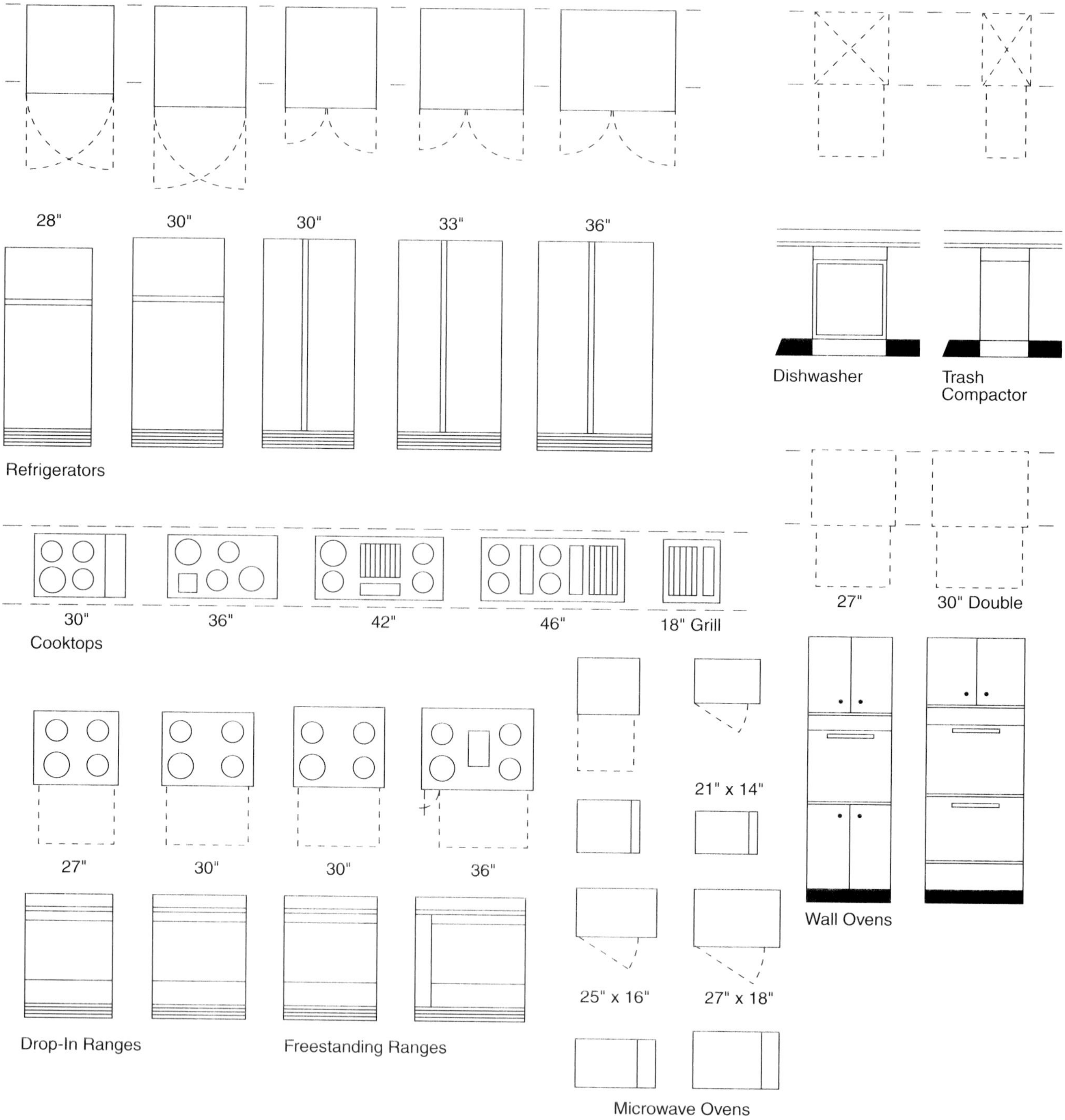

28"   30"   30"   33"   36"

Refrigerators

Dishwasher   Trash Compactor

30"   36"   42"   46"   18" Grill

Cooktops

27"   30" Double

27"   30"   30"   36"

21" x 14"

Wall Ovens

Drop-In Ranges   Freestanding Ranges

25" x 16"   27" x 18"

Microwave Ovens

Planning Grid

Use a photocopier to reproduce the grid at its original size, and then cut out the templates on pages 181–182 to design your new or remodeled kitchen. Grid scale: 1 square equals 1 square foot.

Working with a Pro

Choosing the best professionals to design and build your project makes the entire experience more enjoyable and ensures top-notch results. Whether you're searching for a kitchen designer, architect, or contractor, use the following tactics to track down the best one for you.

BACKGROUND RESEARCH

Gather. Collect the names of professionals to investigate and interview. Ask for recommendations. Identify local references through professional organizations such as the American Institute of Architects (800-242-3837, www.aia.org), the National Kitchen and Bath Association (877-NKBA-PRO, www.nkba.org), and the Remodelers Council of the National Association of Home Builders (800-368-5242, ext. 8216, www.nahb.org).

Explore. Select four to six individuals from each of the professions you plan to use. Call them and ask for references. Contact the references and ask them to recount their experiences.

Evaluate. Based on these references, interview the top three candidates in

each profession and tour some of their finished projects. Savvy architects, designers, and contractors will ask you questions to determine your expectations and needs. You should come away with a feel for the quality of the professional's work and how well your personalities and visions mesh.

MAKE A DECISION

Solicit. To narrow your choices between two or more architects or kitchen designers, it may be worth the additional cost to solicit preliminary drawings from each one. Ask contractors for bids, but don't base your decision on cost alone. Instead weigh what you learned in the interview with the thoroughness of the bid.

Sign up. Before hiring a professional, write up a contract that legally protects you before, during, and after the work is done. Define the scope of the project and fees as specifically as possible. Include a clear description of the work to be done, materials required, and who will supply them. In addition spell out beginning and completion dates and any provisions relating to timelines. Include your total costs (subject to additions and deductions by written change order only) and tie payment to work stages. Be wary of any contractor who asks for a lot of money up front. If certain materials need to be ordered

REMODELING SURVIVAL TIPS

To ensure that the inconveniences of a remodeling project don't turn into major headaches, discuss your concerns with your contractor before work begins and develop a plan to minimize disruption.

- Control dust. Tape a plastic barrier over doorways. Tape off heat registers and change furnace filters daily, especially if drywall is sanded.
- Protect floors. Request that walkways and carpeted areas that lead to the construction zone be covered with drop cloths or plastic runners.
- Reduce noise. Ask workers to arrive and leave at reasonable hours but understand that shorter workdays may lengthen the duration of the project.
- Coordinate schedules. Let the contractor know in advance if there are any times when your house will be off-limits to project work.
- Create a temporary kitchen. Move the refrigerator and the microwave oven to the dining room to reduce problems that come with limited accessibility.

1: Even a modest-size kitchen can benefit from the input of a design professional. This kitchen suffered through multiple well-intentioned but not well-executed renovations. After a designer-contractor recommended removing a wall, the new L-shape kitchen became efficient and effective.

2: An interior designer suggested this vibrant and dramatic backsplash that serves as the focal point of the kitchen. Formed from Italian glass tiles, it reaches from the countertop to the top of the upper cabinets for a cohesive look.

in advance, get a list of those materials and their costs before making a down payment. Kitchens usually require a sizable cash advance to finance appliances and cabinetry.

STAGES AND PHASES

Prepare for your kitchen project by knowing what to expect during the process and how to save money. While no two projects are exactly alike, they normally follow a process similar to the following.

Plan. Determine whether you'll use a design professional. Pin down the design and begin shaping the budget. When shopping for elements, find out how long it will take to receive materials and appliances; figure this into the project schedule. Once your design is complete, select a contractor. Some contractors may suggest alternatives for accomplishing the design. Finish the budget and determine a timeline. Select products and arrange for delivery.

Confer. Invite the key players—architect or designer, contractor, primary subcontractors, and job

supervisor—to your home. Tour your kitchen together and review the project particulars. Establish any ground rules between you and the professionals you hire. One idea is to place a notebook in a prominent location where both you and the crew can jot down comments and questions.

Prepare. Remove your personal belongings from the jobsite. To prevent dust and debris from spreading throughout the house, hang plastic sheeting and seal it securely between the jobsite and the rest of the house.

Demolish. Remove any built-in structures such as cabinetry, counters, islands, or walls that will not be included in the final project. Doing the demolition yourself may save you money. If that's an option you like, discuss your participation with

your contractor during the Plan and Confer stages.

Construct. If you're building an addition, the foundation and framing go up first. Next come windows, plumbing, electrical wiring, and heating, ventilation, and air-conditioning ductwork, followed by insulation, drywall, roofing, and siding. Finish carpentry and electrical connections are next, then the flooring. After that, appliances, light fixtures, and plumbing fixtures are installed. Wood floors can be sanded, stained, and sealed at this stage.

Finish. Walk through the completed project with your contractor and architect, noting any concerns or unfinished details. It's the contractor's responsibility to follow up on your list and complete the project.

Budgeting

and contribute some of your own sweat equity to the project.

CONTROLLING COSTS

If your plans and projects are bigger than your budget, use the following tips to help save money.

Choose materials wisely. Birch cabinets cost two to three times less than solid cherry, and you can personalize them with stain, paint, or stenciling. Buy stock cabinets and customize them with molding.

Get help. Swap jobs with handy neighbors. Throw a party in exchange for some labor. Ask family and friends to help out.

Assist as a general laborer. Consider tackling simple tasks: removing wallpaper, painting, and minor trimwork and cleanup. A cost-plus-fixed-fee contract credits your labor against a contractor's fee.

Act as your own contractor. This is a full-time job—you need to understand the project, the order of work, and building codes if you plan to do it.

Rent the equipment. It's better than buying if you're completing part of the project yourself.

Compare prices. Your contractor gets a discount on many products, but you might pay less if you shop around.

Keep the shape simple. Remember that a square foundation for an addition costs less than one with lots of angles.

Work around objects. Rather than spending the money to move objects such as plumbing stacks, heat runs, and chimneys, work around them. Leave the exterior openings in their original locations.

Do it yourself. If you enjoy working with tools and have a basic knowledge of home construction, consider remodeling your kitchen yourself.

FUNDING SOURCES

Kitchen redos aren't cheap. Fortunately there are many ways to pay.

Savings. If you've socked away enough to fund your project, you're sitting pretty: no waiting, no finance costs, no payments.

Income. By doing a major project in stages, you can pay for a portion of the work over a set period of time. By stretching out the project, you buy time to shop for bargains on big-ticket elements and to do some or all of the work yourself. On the other hand, it prolongs the inconvenience of not having a kitchen, and if you end up dining out you may literally eat up any savings you accrue.

Home equity loan. If you have enough equity in your home to pay for the kitchen you want, you may be able to finance the project with a home equity loan. The loan may be tax-deductible and rates are generally lower than for other consumer loans.

Home equity line of credit. A home equity line of credit is a loan that allows you to borrow up to a preset amount on a revolving credit account that works similarly to a credit card, yet generally with lower rates and tax-deductible interest. You only pay interest on

money as you spend it. Because the cost of a renovation is spread over time as you buy materials and pay contractors, the interest costs for a line of credit should be less than those of a lump-sum loan, all other factors being equal.

Mortgage. If you're planning to remodel a home that you're about to buy, ask your lender about the possibility of getting a mortgage for the price of the home plus the price of the kitchen you desire. The interest you pay is tax-deductible, and the cost will be spread out over the term of the loan.

Credit card. Due to high interest rates on credit cards, use this source of funding only as a last resort. Be careful because a combination of cost overruns and job delays can leave you with a big, high-interest balance to pay.

Combination of sources. Sometimes a patchwork of funding from a variety of sources is the way to go: You might use some savings, pay some as you go, purchase appliances with a special no-interest-for-a-year retail promotion,

---

1: Budgeting is essential to achieve a high-quality, high-end gourmet kitchen like this one. Fortunately there are a variety of financing options, some of which offer tax advantages depending upon your situation.

2: As you plan for your new or remodeled kitchen, budget for those items you consider essential—perhaps a stunning countertop such as this one—and consider what items you might have to sacrifice to afford the "must-haves."

Resources

Consult the following organizations, books, magazines, and websites for additional kitchen design and planning information and inspiration.

ORGANIZATIONS

The National Association of Home Builders
800-368-5242
www.nahb.org
This industry site offers information for consumers to learn more about the home building and remodeling process—from hiring professionals, financing, and contracts to insurance and surviving the process.

The National Kitchen and Bath Association
877-NKBA-PRO
www.nkba.org
Turn to this site to find a design professional in your area and information on industry trends, products, and services. You can request a free consumer workbook, browse designers' answers to common kitchen-related questions, read articles on numerous aspects of kitchen design, and view award-winning kitchens.

BUILDING CODES AND BUILDING OFFICIALS

Building codes are designed to protect the structural integrity of your home, safeguarding your health and safety and that of your family, friends, and anyone who comes in contact with your home. Before you plan any remodeling project, visit the local building department; doing so will help you take your ideas further and may well be the most enlightening time you invest in your project.

Your governing building official and codes will likely be the building department of your town or city

government. If you live outside city limits, this function may be performed at the county level by a clerk or commission. Occasionally county officials don't govern a property, and you'll need to call the state departments of building standards or housing to find a governing official.

Be prepared to tell the official what you're thinking of doing, even if your ideas are rough, and ask what building codes will apply. A rough sketch of the available space and the location of windows, doors, and mechanical systems will make your visit even more productive. Don't be dissuaded if local

codes call for a standard that you can't meet. Ask about exceptions: Many officials are willing to make them to accommodate existing buildings if safety or practicality isn't compromised.

BETTER HOMES AND GARDENS® ONLINE RESOURCES

Visit the Better Homes and Gardens website at www.bhg.com, where you'll find a wealth of ideas and help. Special features on the site include the following:

• **Arrange-a-Room.** Try this interactive tool that allows you to lay out any room in your home.

• **The BHG.com/Home Improvement Encyclopedia.** Go to this page for help with interior and exterior improvement, repair projects and updates, information on do-it-yourself projects, calculators to help you estimate costs and materials, and a tool dictionary. There's also a section of Home Solutions that offers everything from quick fixes to remodeling project ideas.

• **Decorating Gallery.** From design lessons to projects and ideas, you'll find the information you want here.

• **Color-a-Room.** Click on this page to find painting techniques and color choices.

• **Ready, Set, Organize.** Find efficient, inspired storage ideas here.

BOOKS AND MAGAZINES
The following Better Homes and Gardens® publications are available on newsstands and in bookstores. Or order them online at www.bhgbooks.com.

Books
- *Additions: How to Expand Your Home*
- *Additions Planner*
- *Kitchens: Dream It. Plan It. Remodel It.*
- *Kitchens: Your Guide to Planning and Remodeling*
- *Kitchen Planner*
- *Remodeling Idea File*

Magazines
- *Better Homes and Gardens*®
- *Country Home*®
- *Dream Kitchens*®
- *Kitchen & Bath Ideas*
- *Kitchen & Bath Products Guide*
- *Kitchen Planning Guide*
- *Remodel*
- *Remodeling Products Guide*
- *Renovation Style*
- *Traditional Home*®
- *Traditional Home Decorator Showcase*

BUILDING CODE CONSISTENCY

Cities, towns, and municipalities are free to choose the building codes they adhere to, which means what's permissible in one location isn't necessarily OK in another. In recent years, however, three of the country's largest building code organizations—The International Conference of Building Officials (ICBO), the Building Officials and Code Administrators (BOCA), and the Southern Building Code Council International, Inc. (SBCC)—have combined forces to create the International Code Council (ICC). The ICC has a coordinated, comprehensive set of building codes, called I-Codes, to serve the nation. Municipalities across the country have been quickly adopting the I-Codes, which were completed in 2000. If you're remodeling a part of your home, three of the ICC codes might apply to your project: the building, residential, and zoning codes. In general, the I-Codes are less restrictive with some issues, such as ceiling height (if a standard door can open into the space, it's OK), and more conservative with respect to safety issues, such as requiring egress windows. For more information, contact your local building department or the ICC at www.iccsafe.org. The I-Codes—or e-codes—are available online for a fee.

An inspired kitchen design outfitted with high-quality materials and appliances should be the result of your research into the options for kitchen appliances, cabinetry, surface materials, and amenities.

MANUFACTURER RESOURCES AND ONLINE TOOLS

These online and interactive design tools allow you to fine-tune your kitchen planning and remodeling ideas. Some sites allow you to drop product choices into room style settings, and then change the color of the walls and features to preview various combinations. Other sites feature extensive "galleries" of ideas. Use these sites to get started. Or call the manufacturers directly to find what products are available in your area.

APPLIANCES
- Amana Appliances, 800-843-0304, www.amana.com
- Dacor, 800-793-0093, www.dacor.com
- DCS (Dynamic Cooking Systems, Inc.), 800-433-8466, www.dcsappliances.com
- Fisher & Paykel Appliances, Inc., 888-936-7872, www.fisherpaykel.com
- Frigidaire Home Products, 800-374-4432, www.frigidaire.com
- GE Appliances, 800-626-2005, www.geappliances.com
- Jenn-Air, 800-688-1100, www.jennair.com
- Kenmore, by Sears, 888-349-4358, www.kenmore.com
- KitchenAid, 800-422-1230, www.kitchenaid.com
- Sub-Zero, 800-222-7820, www.subzero.com
- Thermador, 800-656-9226, www.thermador.com
- Viking Range Corp., 888-845-4641, www.vikingrange.com

CABINETRY
- KraftMaid Cabinetry, 888-562-7744, www.kraftmaid.com
- Merillat Industries, www.merillat.com
- Plain & Fancy Custom Cabinetry, 800-447-9006, www.plainfancycabinetry.com
- Rutt HandCrafted Cabinetry, LLC, 717-351-1700, www.rutt.net
- SieMatic, www.siematic.com

FLOORING
- Armstrong Floors, 800-233-3823, www.armstrongfloors.com
- Congoleum Floors, 800-274-3266, www.congoleum.com

SINKS AND FAUCETS
- Delta Faucet Company, 800-345-3358, www.deltafaucet.com
- Elkay, 630-574-8484, www.elkay.com
- Kohler, 800-456-4537, www.kohler.com
- Moen, 800-BUY-MOEN, www.moen.com

WINDOW MANUFACTURERS
- Andersen Windows, 888-888-7020, www.andersonwindows.com
- Hy-Lite Products (block glass), www.hy-lite.com
- Jeld-Wen, Inc., 800-535-3936, www.jeld-wen.com
- Kolbe & Kolbe Millwork Co., Inc., 715-842-5666, www.kolbekolbe.com
- Marvin Windows and Doors, 888-537-7828, www.marvin.com
- Peachtree Doors and Windows, www.peach99.com
- Pella Windows, www.pella.com
- Pozzi Wood Windows, www.pozzi.com
- Quantum Windows & Doors, Inc., 800-287-6650, www.quantumwindows.com
- Velux-America (skylights), 800-888-3589, www.veluxusa.com
- Weather Shield Windows & Doors, 800-222-2995, www.weathershield.com

Index